FUCK IT: THE HEALTH ,WEALTH, LOVE , HAPPINESS AND SUCCESS

ARVIND UPADHYAY

Made with ♥ on the Notion Press Platform
www.notionpress.com

"In a world where so many teach and very few actually lead, **arvind upadhyay: books** I Introduction don't know why you're reading this book. Maybe you're waiting in the airport, and the book cover caught your attention. You're flipping through this book wondering whether you should pick it up or not. Or maybe a friend of yours gave you this book. Possibly, you're one of my fans on social media and familiar with who I am. No. I don't know why you're reading this book. One thing I do know is that if you're reading this book, you want more. You see, many people are not interested in improving their life in any shape or form. Very often, they feel stuck, as if they don't have the power to change and accept life as is. But YOU are different. You believe in something else. You believe you have the desire to change, the ability to succeed, and that you can be a better version of you. You believe you have the power to unlock your destiny. Now, you might have read a lot of different books on success, selfimprovement, wealth, and business already. This book may not be your first "personal development rodeo." Even though you learn a lot from different books and they teach you many different things, let me ask you a question. Do you feel deep down there's still a missing piece? Like you're putting together a jigsaw puzzle, and you have some pieces, but you never get to see the whole picture? You're looking for that missing link. You're looking for that piece of information that connects all the dots. You're looking for that key that unlocks everything else for you. You're looking for that missing link. You're looking for that piece of information that connects all the dots. You're looking for that key that unlocks everything else for you. If that's you, then my goal is to give you that key. I hope that this book will not only give you a new perspective, but more importantly, a road map to implement everything you've learned in the past and to connect those learnings in a clear, concise manner. Chances are, if you've read other books, what I'm sharing with you is nothing you haven't heard of before. I don't claim to be a super original thinker. The truth is, I think originality is highly overrated. You can always tell who the pioneer is when they are lying on the ground with arrows in their back. No, I'm not an original thinker. I'm an entrepreneur. I'm a synthesizer. I take ideas, make them better, and execute them better than most. Absorb what is useful, discard what is not, add what is uniquely your own. BRUCE LEE Most books will tell you to do this and don't do that; don't do this and do that instead. That's not what I'm here to do. This book is here to share with you a new perspective and a system that shows you how to think differently. My challenge as an educator is to change the way you think. Changing the way you think will alter the way you do things. The exciting part for me is that inevitably the way you do things will force you to produce different results. Now, there will be information that I share that you may or may not agree with. That's perfectly fine. Everything I teach comes from my experience, so it doesn't make it right. It doesn't make it wrong either; it just makes it my experience. All I can do is come from my own experience. I ask that you read this book cafeteria-style. Take what seems useful and implement it. If it works, great—keep it. If it doesn't work, that's okay too— throw it away. No hard feelings. That's how I believe we all should learn.I Introduction don't know why you're reading this book. Maybe you're waiting in the airport, and the book cover caught your attention. You're flipping through this book wondering whether you should pick it up or not. Or maybe a friend of yours gave you this book. Possibly, you're one of my fans on social media and familiar with who I am. No. I don't know why you're reading this book. One thing I do know is that if you're reading this book, you want more. You see, many people are not interested in improving their life in any shape or form. Very often, they feel stuck, as if they don't have the power to change and accept life as is. But YOU are different. You believe in something else. You believe you have the desire to change, the ability to succeed, and that you can be a better version of you. You believe you have the power to unlock your destiny. Now, you might have read a lot of different books on success, selfimprovement, wealth, and business already. This book may not be your first "personal development rodeo." Even though you learn a lot from different books and they teach you many different things, let me ask you a question. Do you feel deep down there's still a missing piece? Like you're putting together a jigsaw puzzle, and you have some pieces, but you never get to see the whole picture? You're looking for that missing link. You're looking for that piece of information that connects all the dots. You're looking for that key that unlocks everything else for you. You're looking for that missing link. You're looking for that piece of information that connects all the dots. You're looking for that key that unlocks everything else for you. If that's you, then my goal is to give you that key. I hope that this book will not only give you a new perspective, but more importantly, a road map to implement everything you've learned in the past and to connect those learnings in a clear, concise manner. Chances are, if you've read other books, what I'm sharing with you is nothing you haven't heard of before.

I've heard countless stories of college students coming out of school, and they can't get a job. Even though they've studied in school for four years, their employers will tell them in interviews that they don't have enough experience. So they go back to school and get further into debt; they get an MBA or a second degree and work even harder. Now when they sit across the table from the employer, they say they have too much experience. Sometimes, the jobs they prepare to get will become extinct by the time they get out of school. So what do you do? They feel handcuffed even though they did what they were supposed to do. It's not just students who are struggling. Entrepreneurs come up to me and share their pain. They have trouble getting their products noticed, they can't get anything to sell, their operating costs are going up, and costs are rising, and there's more on the line. Technology is lowering the barrier to entry and making the marketplace more competitive than ever. Overall, it's just getting more challenging to run a business. Even successful entrepreneurs who have "made it" come up to me and share with me their concerns about staying in business. They're not sure if the success they've built is going to last or how to sustain their success or how to take it to the next level. New technologies are going to come and wipe out their entire business. They know social media is powerful, and they know a new way of doing business is emerging, but they're not sure how to adapt to this change. Now that they've achieved a taste of financial success, they understand that the name of the game is not getting rich; the name of the game is staying rich. WHAT YOU'LL GET FROM THIS BOOK In my past twenty years of business and life, I've picked up key lessons and principles that have helped turn me from a poor Asian immigrant with $150,000 in debt to a leader of a global organization. When I've followed these lessons, I've succeeded. When I've disobeyed these principles, I've failed. So whether you want to excel in your career, carve out a path on your own, or build a company that lasts, you'll find useful ideas here. First, you'll get to know me very well. You'll see how I wasn't given anything in life and how I was able to rise from nothing to something. From my journey, one key concept that has guided my philosophy about financial success is the Wealth Triangle. In chapter 1, I'll introduce you to the Wealth Triangle and why (contrary to popular belief) starting a business is a horrible first step to achieving wealth and success. There are three steps to the Wealth Triangle—and most people do things in the wrong order. I'll show you the right sequence to achieve the milestones in the Wealth Triangle. I'll introduce you to the six universal Wealth Archetypes. These are archetypes and profiles that will help you identify your relationship with money and where you are on your wealth journey. After you get clarity on where you are, you'll be able to start the first step of the Wealth Triangle. The first step of the Wealth Triangle is attaining the High-Income Skill that will help you pay the bills. It's a skill that will help you become recession proof. Most successful CEOs and entrepreneurs didn't start with a business as their first step; they began with a High-Income Skill. In chapter 3, you'll learn about the power of a High-Income Skill and why debt problems are skill problems in disguise. Even with a High-Income Skill, there is a metaskill most people don't have. That skill is the art of achieving maximum productivity. In chapter 5, you'll learn how to achieve maximum results in minimum time. This chapter won't be a chapter on time management—far from it. You'll see why productivity is self-mastery, and you'll see how a few simple adjustments to your current routine could multiply your results. After achieving maximum personal productivity, you'll learn how to achieve maximum financial productivity. Whether you want to move up in your company, become your own boss, or empower your employees with a powerful skill, this chapter will show you a new brand of sales.

Contents

1

BIASES AND BLUNDERS

Suppose that you are thinking about which one would work better as a coffee table in your living room. What would you say are the dimensions of the two tables? Take a guess at the ratio of the length to the width of each. Just eyeball it. If you are like most people, you think that the table on the left is much longer and narrower than the one on the right. Typical guesses are that the ratio of the length to the width is 3:1 for the left table and 1.5:1 for the right table. Now take out a ruler and measure each table. You will find that the two table tops are identical. Measure them until you are convinced, because this is a case where seeing is not believing. (When Thaler showed this example to Sunstein at their usual lunch haunt, Sunstein grabbed his chopstick to check.) What should we conclude from this example? If you see the left table as longer and thinner than the right one, you are certifiably human. There is nothing wrong with you (well, at least not that we can detect from this test). Still, your judgment in this task was biased, and predictably so. No one thinks that the right table is thinner! Not only were you wrong; you were probably confident that you were right. If you like, you can put this visual to good use when you encounter others who are equally human and who are disposed to gamble away their money, say, at a bar. Now consider Figure 1.2. Do these two shapes look the same or different? Again, if you are human, and have decent vision, you probably see these shapes as being identical, as they are. But these two shapes are just the table tops from Figure 1.1, removed from their legs and reoriented.

the key insight that behavioral economists have borrowed from psychologists. Normally the human mind works remarkably well. We can recognize people we have not seen in years, understand the complexities of our native language, and run down a flight of stairs without falling. Some of us can speak twelve languages, improve the fanciest computers, and/or create the theory of relativity. However, even Einstein would probably be fooled by those tables. That does not mean something is wrong with us as humans, but it does mean that our understanding of human behavior can be improved by appreciating how people systematically go wrong. To obtain that understanding, we need to explore some aspects of human thinking. Knowing something about the visual system allowed Roger Shepard (1990), a psychologist and artist, to draw those deceptive tables. He knew what to draw to lead our mind astray. Knowing something about the cognitive system has allowed others to discover systematic biases in the way we think. How We Think: Two Systems The workings of the human brain are more than a bit befuddling. How can we be so ingenious at some tasks and so clueless at others? Beethoven wrote his incredible ninth symphony while he was deaf, but we would not be at all surprised if we learned that he often misplaced his house keys. How can people be simultaneously so smart and so dumb? Many psychologists and neuroscientists have been converging on a description of the brain's functioning that helps us make sense of these seeming contradictions. The approach involves a distinction between two kinds of thinking, one that is intuitive and automatic, and another that is reflective and rational.1 We will call the first the Automatic System and the second the Reflective System. (In the psychology literature, these two systems are sometimes referred to as System 1 and System 2, respectively.) The key features of each system are shown in Table 1.1. The Automatic System is rapid and is or feels instinctive, and it does not involve what we usually associate with the word thinking. When you duck because a ball is thrown at you unexpectedly, or get nervous when your airplane hits turbulence, or smile when you see a cute puppy, you are using

Table 1.1 Two cognitive systems Automatic System Reflective System Uncontrolled Controlled Effortless Effortful Associative Deductive Fast Slow Unconscious Self-aware Skilled Rule-following

your Automatic System. Brain scientists are able to say that the activities of the Automatic System are associated with the oldest parts of the brain, the parts we share with lizards (as well as puppies).2 The Reflective System is more deliberate and self-conscious. We use the Reflective System when we are asked, "How much is 411 times 37?" Most people are also likely to use the Reflective System when deciding which route to take for a trip and whether to go to law school or business school. When we are writing this book we are (mostly) using our Reflective Systems, but sometimes ideas pop into our heads when we are in the shower or taking a walk and not thinking at all about the book, and these probably are coming from our Automatic Systems. (Voters, by the way, seem to rely primarily on their Automatic System.3 A candidate who makes a bad first impression, or who tries to win votes by complex arguments and statistical demonstrations, may well run into trouble.)* Most Americans have an Automatic System reaction to a temperature given in Fahrenheit but have to use their Reflective System to process a temperature given in Celsius; for Europeans, the opposite is true. People speak their native languages using their Automatic Systems and tend to struggle to speak another language using their Reflective Systems. Being truly bilingual means that you speak two languages using the Automatic System. Accomplished chess players and professional athletes have pretty fancy intuitions; their Automatic Systems allow them to size up complex situations rapidly and to respond with both amazing accuracy and exceptional speed. One way to think about all this is that the Automatic System is your gut reaction and the Reflective System is your conscious thought. Gut feelings can be quite accurate, but we often make mistakes because we rely too much on our Automatic System. The Automatic System says that "the airplane is shaking, I'm going to die," while the Reflective System responds, "Planes are very safe!" The Automatic System says, "That big dog is going to hurt me," and the Reflective System replies, "Most pets are quite sweet." (In both cases, the Automatic System is squawking all the time.) The Automatic System starts out with no idea how to play golf or tennis. Note, however, that countless hours of practice enable an accomplished golfer to avoid reflection and to rely on her Automatic System—so much so that good golfers, like other good athletes, know the hazards of "thinking too much" and might well do better to "trust the gut," or "just do it." The Automatic System can be trained with lots of repetition—but such training takes a lot of time and effort. One reason why teenagers are such risky drivers is that their Automatic Systems have not had much practice, and using the Reflective System is much slower. To see how intuitive thinking works, try the following little test. For each of the three questions, begin by writing down the first answer that comes to your mind. Then pause to reflect. 1. A bat and ball cost $1.10 in total. The bat costs $1.00 more than the ball. How much does the ball cost? _______ cents 2. If it takes 5 machines 5 minutes to make 5 widgets, how long would it take 100 machines to make

100 widgets? _______ minutes 3. In a lake, there is a patch of lily pads. Every day, the patch doubles in size. If it takes 48 days for the patch to cover the entire lake, how long would it take for the patch to cover half of the lake? _______ days What were your initial answers? Most people say 10 cents, 100 minutes, and 24 days. But all these answers are wrong. If you think for a minute, you will see why. If the ball costs 10 cents and the bat costs one dollar more than the ball, meaning $1.10, then together they cost $1.20, not $1.10. No one who bothers to check whether his initial answer of 10 cents could possibly be right would give that as an answer, but research by Shane Frederick (2005) (who calls this series of questions the cognitive reflection test) finds that these are the most popular answers even among bright college students. The correct answers are 5 cents, 5 minutes, and 47 days, but you knew that, or at least your Reflective System did if you bothered to consult it. Econs never make an important decision without checking with their Reflective Systems (if they have time). But Humans sometimes go with the answer the lizard inside is giving without pausing to think. If you are a television fan, think of Mr. Spock of Star Trek fame as someone whose Reflective System is always in control. (Captain Kirk: "You'd make a splendid computer, Mr. Spock." Mr. Spock: "That is very kind of you, Captain!") In contrast, Homer Simpson seems to have forgotten where he put his Reflective System. (In a commentary on gun control, Homer once replied to a gun store clerk who informed him of a mandatory five-day waiting period before buying a weapon, "Five days? But I'm mad now!") One of our major goals in this book is to see how the world might be made easier, or safer, for the Homers among us (and the Homer lurking somewhere in each of us). If people can rely on their Automatic Systems without getting into terrible trouble, their lives should be easier, better, and longer. Rules of Thumb Most of us are busy, our lives are complicated, and we can't spend all our time thinking and analyzing everything. When we have to make judgments, such as guessing Angelina Jolie's age or the distance between Cleveland and Philadelphia, we use simple rules of thumb to help us. We use rules of thumb because most of the time they are quick and useful. In fact, there is a great collection edited by Tom Parker titled Rules of Thumb. Parker wrote the book by asking friends to send him good rules of thumb. For example, "One ostrich egg will serve 24 people for brunch." "Ten people will raise the temperature of an average size room by one degree per hour." And one to which we will return: "No more than 25 percent of the guests at a university dinner party can come from the economics department without

spoiling the conversation."

Although rules of thumb can be very helpful, their use can also lead to systematic biases. This insight, first developed decades ago by two Israeli psychologists, Amos Tversky and Daniel Kahneman (1974), has changed the way psychologists (and eventually economists) think about thinking. Their original work identified three heuristics, or rules of thumb—anchoring, availability, and representativeness—and the biases that are associated with each. Their research program has come to be known as the "heuristics and biases" approach to the study of human judgment. More recently, psychologists have come to understand that these heuristics and biases emerge from the interplay between the Automatic System and the Reflective System. Let's see how. Anchoring Suppose we are asked to guess the population of Milwaukee, a city about two hours north of Chicago, where we live. Neither of us knows much about Milwaukee, but we think that it is the biggest city in Wisconsin. How should we go about guessing? Well, one thing we could do is start with something we do know, which is the population of Chicago, roughly three million. So we might think, Milwaukee is a major city, but clearly not as big as Chicago, so, hmmm, maybe it is one-third the size, say one million. Now consider someone from Green Bay, Wisconsin, who is asked the same question. She also doesn't know the answer, but she does know that Green Bay has about one hundred thousand people and knows that Milwaukee is larger, so guesses, say, three times larger—three hundred thousand. This process is called "anchoring and adjustment." You start with some anchor, the number you know, and adjust in the direction you think is appropriate. So far, so good. The bias occurs because the adjustments are typically insufficient. Experiments repeatedly show that, in problems similar to our example, people from Chicago are likely to make a high guess (based on their high anchor) while those from Green Bay guess low (based on their low anchor). As it happens, Milwaukee has about 580,000 people.4 Even obviously irrelevant anchors creep into the decision-making process. Try this one yourself. Take the last three digits of your phone number and add two hundred. Write the number down. Now, when do you think Attila the Hun sacked Europe? Was it before or after that year? What is your best guess? (We will give you one hint: It was after the birth of Jesus.) Even if you do not know much about European history, you do know enough to know that whenever Attila did whatever he did, the date has nothing to do with your phone number. Still, when we conduct this experiment with our students, we get answers that are more than three hundred years later from students who start with high anchors rather than low ones. (The right answer is 411.) Anchors can even influence how you think your life is going. In one experiment, college students were asked two questions: (a) How happy are you? (b) How often are you dating? When the two questions were asked in this order the correlation between the two questions was quite low (.11). But when the question order was reversed, so that the dating question was asked first, the correlation jumped to .62. Apparently, when prompted by the dating question, the students use what might be called the "dating heuristic" to answer the question about how happy they are. "Gee, I can't remember when I last had a date! I must be miserable." Similar results can be obtained from married couples if the dating question is replaced by a lovemaking question.5 In the language of this book, anchors serve as nudges. We can influence the figure you will choose in a particular situation by ever-so-subtly suggesting a starting point for your thought process. When charities ask you for a donation, they typically offer you a range of options such as $100, $250, $1,000, $5,000, or "other." If the charity's fund-raisers have an idea of what they are doing, these values are not picked at random, because the options influence the amount of money people decide to donate. People will give more if the options are $100, $250, $1,000, and $5,000, than if the options are $50, $75, $100, and $150. In many domains, the evidence shows that, within reason, the more you ask for, the more you tend to get. Lawyers who sue cigarette companies often win astronomical amounts, in part because they have successfully induced juries to anchor on multimillion-dollar figures. Clever negotiators often get amazing deals for their clients by producing an opening offer that makes their adversary thrilled to pay half that very high amount. Availability How much should you worry about hurricanes, nuclear power, terrorism, mad cow disease, alligator attacks, or avian flu? And how much care should you take in avoiding risks associated with each? What, exactly, should you do to prevent the kinds of dangers that you face in ordinary life? In answering questions of this kind, most people use what is called the availability heuristic. They assess the likelihood of risks by asking how readily examples come to mind. If people can easily think of relevant examples, they are far more likely to be frightened and concerned than if they cannot. A risk that is familiar, like that associated with terrorism in the aftermath of 9/11, will be seen as more serious than a risk that is less familiar, like that associated with sunbathing or hotter summers. Homicides are more available than suicides, and so people tend to believe, wrongly, that more people die from homicide. Accessibility and salience are closely related to availability, and they are important as well. If you have personally experienced a serious earthquake, you're more likely to believe that an earthquake is likely than if you read about it in a weekly magazine. Thus vivid and easily imagined causes of death (for example, tornadoes) often receive inflated estimates of probability, and less-vivid causes (for example, asthma attacks) receive low estimates, even if they occur with a far greater frequency (here a factor of twenty). So, too, recent events have a greater impact on our behavior, and on our fears, than earlier ones. In all these highly available examples, the Automatic System is keenly aware of the risk (perhaps too keenly), without having to resort to any tables of boring statistics. The availability heuristic helps to explain much risk-related behavior, including both public and private decisions to take precautions. Whether people buy insurance for natural disasters is greatly affected by recent experiences.6 In the aftermath of an earthquake, purchases of new earthquake insurance policies rise sharply—but purchases decline steadily from that point, as vivid memories recede. If floods have not occurred in the immediate past, people who live on floodplains are far less likely to purchase insurance. And people who know someone who has experienced a flood are more likely to buy flood insurance for themselves, regardless of the flood risk they actually face. Biased assessments of risk can perversely influence how we prepare for and respond to crises, business choices, and the political process. When Internet stocks have done very well, people might well buy Internet stocks,even if by that point they've become a bad investment. Or suppose that people falsely think that some risks (a nuclear power accident) are high, whereas others (a stroke) are relatively low. Such misperceptions can affect policy, because governments are likely to allocate their resources in a way that fits with people's fears rather than in response to the most likely danger. When "availability bias" is at work, both private and public decisions may be improved if judgments can be nudged back in the direction of true probabilities. A good way to increase people's fear of a bad outcome is to remind them of a related incident in which things went wrong; a good way to increase people's confidence is to remind them of a similar situation in which everything worked out for the best. The pervasive problems are that easily remembered events may inflate people's probability judgments, and that if no such events come to mind, their judgments of likelihoods might be distorted downward. Representativeness The third of the original three heuristics bears an unwieldy name: representativeness.

Think of it as the similarity heuristic. The idea is that when asked to judge how likely it is that A belongs to category B, people (and especially their Automatic Systems) answer by asking themselves how similar A is to their image or stereotype of B (that is, how "representative" A is of B). Like the other two heuristics we have discussed, this one is used because it often works. We think a 6-foot-8-inch African-American man is more likely to be a professional basketball player than a 5-foot-6-inch Jewish guy because there are lots of tall black basketball players and not many short Jewish ones (at least not these days). Stereotypes are sometimes right! Again, biases can creep in when similarity and frequency diverge. The most famous demonstration of such biases involves the case of a hypothetical woman named Linda. In this experiment, subjects were told the following: "Linda is thirty-one years old, single, outspoken, and very bright. She majored in philosophy. As a student, she was deeply concerned with issues of discrimination and social justice and also participated in antinuclear demonstrations." Then people were asked to rank, in order of the probability of their occurrence, eight possible futures for Linda. The two crucial answers were "bank teller" and "bank teller and active in the feminist movement." Most people said that Linda was less likely to be a bank teller than to be a bank teller and active in the feminist movement. This is an obvious logical mistake. It is, of course, not logically possible for any two events to be more likely than one of them alone. It just has to be the case that Linda is more likely to be a bank teller than a feminist bank teller, because all feminist bank tellers are bank tellers. The error stems from the use of the representativeness heuristic: Linda's description seems to match "bank teller and active in the feminist movement" far better than "bank teller." As Stephen Jay Gould (1991) once observed, "I know [the right answer], yet a little homunculus in my head continues to jump up and down, shouting at me—'but she can't just be a bank teller; read the description!'" Gould's homunculus is the Automatic System in action. Use of the representativeness heuristic can cause serious misperceptions of patterns in everyday life. When events are determined by chance, such as a sequence of coin tosses, people expect the resulting string of heads and tails to be representative of what they think of as random. Unfortunately, people do not have accurate perceptions of what random sequences look like. When they see the outcomes of random processes, they often detect patterns that they think have great meaning but in fact are just due to chance. You might flip a coin three times, see it come up heads every time, and conclude that there is something funny about the coin. But the fact is that if you flip any coin a lot, it won't be so unusual to see three heads in a row. (Try it and you'll see. As a little test, Sunstein, having just finished this paragraph, flipped a regular penny three times—and got heads every time. He was amazed. He shouldn't have been.) A less trivial example, from the Cornell psychologist Tom Gilovich (1991), comes from the experience of London residents during the German bombing campaigns of World War II. London newspapers published maps, such as the one shown in Figure 1.3, displaying the location of the strikes from German V-1 and V-2 missiles that landed in central London. As you can see, the pattern does not seem at all random. Bombs appear to be clustered around the River Thames and also in the northwest sector of the map. People in London expressed concern at the time because the pattern seemed to suggest that the Germans could aim their bombs with great precision. Some Londoners even speculated that the blank spaces were probably the neighborhoods where German spies lived. They were wrong. In fact the Germans could do no better than aim their bombs at Central London and hope for the best. A detailed statistical analysis of the dispersion of the location of the bomb strikes determined that within London the distribution of bomb strikes was indeed random. Still, the location of the bomb strikes does not look random. What is going on here? We often see patterns because we construct our informal tests only after looking at the evidence. The World War II example is an excellent illustration of this problem. Suppose we divide the map into quadrants, as in Figure 1.4a. If we then do a formal statistical test—or, for the less statistically inclined, just count the number of hits in each quadrant— we do find evidence of a nonrandom pattern. However, nothing in nature suggests that this is the right way to test for randomness. Suppose instead we form the quadrants diagonally as in Figure 1.4b. We are now unable to reject the hypothesis that the bombs land at random. Unfortunately, we do not subject our own perceptions to such rigorous alternative testing. Gilovich (with colleagues Vallone and Tversky [1985]) is also responsible for perhaps the most famous (or infamous) example of misperception of randomness, namely the widely held view among basketball fans that there is a strong pattern of "streak shooting." We will not go into this in detail, because our experience tells us that the cognitive illusion here is so powerful that most people (influenced by their Automatic System) are unwilling even to consider the possibility that their strongly held beliefs might be wrong. But here is the short version. Most basketball fans think that a player is more likely to make his next shot if he has made his last shot, or even better, his last few shots. Players who have hit a few shots in a row, or even most of their recent shots, are said to have a "hot hand," which is taken by all sports announcers to be a good signal about the future. Passing the ball to the player who is hot is taken to be an obvious bit of good strategy. It turns out that the "hot hand" is just a myth. Players who have made their last few shots are no more likely to make their next shot (actually a bit less likely). Really. Once people are told these facts, they quickly start forming alternative versions of the hot-hand theory. Maybe the defense adjusts and guards the "hot" player more closely. Maybe the hot player adjusts and starts taking harder shots. These are fine observations that need to be investigated. But notice that, before seeing the data, when fans were asked about actual shooting percentages after a series of made shots, they routinely subscribed to the hot-hand theory—no qualifiers were thought necessary. Many researchers have been so sure that the original Gilovich results were wrong that they set out to find the hot hand. To date, no one has found it.7 Jay Koehler and Caryn Conley (2003) performed a particularly clean test using the annual three-point shooting contest held at the National Basketball Association All-Star Game. In this contest, the players (among the best three-point shooters in the league) take a series of shots from behind the three-point shooting arc. Their goal is to make as many shots as possible in sixty seconds. Without any defense or alternative shots, this would seem to be an ideal situation in which to observe the hot hand. However, as in the original study, there was no evidence of any streakiness. This absence of streak shooting did not stop the announcers from detecting sudden temperature variations in the players. ("Dana Baros is hot!" "Legler is on fire!") But these outbursts by the announcers had no predictive power. Before the announcers spoke of hotness, the players had made 80.5 percent of their three previous shots. After the hotness pronouncements, players made only 55.2 percent—not significantly better than their overall shooting percentage in the contest, 53.9 percent. Of course, it is no great problem if basketball fans are confused about what they see when they are watching games on television. But the same cognitive biases occur in other, more weighty domains. Consider the phenomenon of "cancer clusters." These can cause a great deal of private and public consternation, and they often attract sustained investigations, designed to see what on earth (or elsewhere) could possibly have caused a sudden and otherwise inexplicable outbreak of cancer cases. Suppose that in a particular neighborhood we find an apparently elevated cancer rate— maybe ten people, in a group of five hundred, have been diagnosed with cancer within the same six-month period. Maybe all ten people live within three blocks of one another. And in fact, American officials receive reports of more than one thousand suspected cancer clusters every year, with many of these suspected clusters investigated further for a possible "epidemic."8 The problem is that in a population of three hundred million, it is inevitable that certain neighborhoods will see unusually high cancer rates within any one-year period. The resulting "cancer clusters" may be products of random fluctuations. Nonetheless, people insist that they could not possibly occur by chance. They get scared, and sometimes government wrongly intervenes on their behalf. Mostly, though, there is thankfully nothing to worry about, except for the fact that the use of the representativeness heuristic can cause people to confuse random fluctuations with causal patterns. Optimism and Overconfidence Before the start of Thaler's class in Managerial Decision Making, students fill out an anonymous survey on the course Web site. One of the questions is "In which decile do you expect to fall in the distribution of grades in this class?" Students can check the top 10 percent, the second 10 percent, and so forth. Since these are mba students, they are presumably well aware that in any distribution, half the population will be in the top 50 percent and half in the bottom. And only 10 percent of the class can, in fact, end up in the top decile.

Nevertheless, the results of this survey reveal a high degree of unrealistic optimism about performance in the class. Typically less than 5 percent of the class expects their performance to be below the median (the 50th percentile) and more than half the class expects to perform in one of the top two deciles. Invariably, the largest group of students put themselves in the second decile. We think this is most likely explained by modesty. They really think they will end up in the top decile, but are too modest to say so. MBA students are not the only ones overconfident about their abilities. The "above average" effect is pervasive. Ninety percent of all drivers think they are above average behind the wheel, even if they don't live in Lake Wobegon. And nearly everyone (including some who are rarely seen smiling) thinks he has an above-average sense of humor. (That is because they know what is funny!) This applies to professors, too. About 94 percent of professors at a large university were found to believe that they are better than the average professor, and there is every reason to think that such overconfidence applies to professors in general.9 (Yes, we admit to this particular failing.)

People are unrealistically optimistic even when the stakes are high. About 50 percent of marriages end in divorce, and this is a statistic most people have heard. But around the time of the ceremony, almost all couples believe that there is approximately a zero percent chance that their marriage will end in divorce—even those who have already been divorced!10 (Second marriage, Samuel Johnson once quipped, "is the triumph of hope over experience.") A similar point applies to entrepreneurs starting new businesses, where the failure rate is at least 50 percent. In one survey of people starting new businesses (typically small businesses, such as contracting firms, restaurants, and salons), respondents were asked two questions: (a) What do you think is the chance of success for a typical business like yours? (b) What is your chance of success? The most common answers to these questions were 50 percent and 90 percent, respectively, and many said 100 percent to the second question.11 Unrealistic optimism can explain a lot of individual risk taking, especially in the domain of risks to life and health. Asked to envision their future, students typically say that they are far less likely than their classmates to be fired from a job, to have a heart attack or get cancer, to be divorced after a few years of marriage, or to have a drinking problem. Gay men systematically underestimate the chance that they will contract AIDS, even though they know about AIDS risks in general. Older people underestimate the likelihood that they will be in a car accident or suffer major diseases. Smokers are aware of the statistical risks, and often even exaggerate them, but most believe that they are less likely to be diagnosed with lung cancer and heart disease than most nonsmokers. Lotteries are successful partly because of unrealistic optimism.12 Unrealistic optimism is a pervasive feature of human life; it characterizes most people in most social categories. When they overestimate their personal immunity from harm, people may fail to take sensible preventive steps. If people are running risks because of unrealistic optimism, they might be able to benefit from a nudge. In fact, we have already mentioned one possibility: if people are reminded of a bad event, they may not continue to be so optimistic. Gains and Losses People hate losses (and their Automatic Systems can get pretty emotional about them). Roughly speaking, losing something makes you twice as miserable as gaining the same thing makes you happy. In more technical language, people are "loss averse." How do we know this? Consider a simple experiment.13 Half the students in a class are given coffee mugs with the insignia of their home university embossed on it. The students who do not get a mug are asked to examine their neighbor's mugs. Then mug owners are invited to sell their mugs and nonowners are invited to buy them. They do so by answering the question "At each of the following prices, indicate whether you would be willing to (give up your mug/buy a mug)." The results show that those with mugs demand roughly twice as much to give up their mugs as others are willing to pay to get one. Thousands of mugs have been used in dozens of replications of this experiment, but the results are nearly always the same. Once I have a mug, I don't want to give it up. But if I don't have one, I don't feel an urgent need to buy one. What this means is that people do not assign specific values to objects. When they have to give something up, they are hurt more than they are pleased if they acquire the very same thing. It is also possible to measure loss aversion with gambles. Suppose I ask you whether you want to make a bet. Heads you win $X, tails you lose $100. How much does X have to be for you to take the bet? For most people, the answer to this question is somewhere around $200. This implies that the prospect of winning $200 just offsets the prospect of losing $100. Loss aversion helps produce inertia, meaning a strong desire to stick with your current holdings. If you are reluctant to give up what you have because you do not want to incur losses, then you will turn down trades you might have otherwise made. In another experiment, half the students in a class received coffee mugs (of course) and half got large chocolate bars. The mugs and the chocolate cost about the same, and in pretests students were as likely to choose one as the other. Yet when offered the opportunity to switch from a mug to a candy bar or vice versa, only one in ten switched. As we will see, loss aversion operates as a kind of cognitive nudge, pressing us not to make changes, even when changes are very much in our interests. Status Quo Bias Loss aversion is not the only reason for inertia. For lots of reasons, people have a more general tendency to stick with their current situation. This phenomenon, which William Samuelson and Richard Zeckhauser (1988) have dubbed the "status quo bias," has been demonstrated in numerous situations. Most teachers know that students tend to sit in the same seats in class, even without a seating chart. But status quo bias can occur even when the stakes are much larger, and it can get us into a lot of trouble. For example, in retirement savings plans, such as 401(k)s, most participants pick an asset allocation and then forget about it. In one study conducted in the late 1980s, participants in tiaa-cref, the pension plan of many college professors, the median number of changes in the asset allocation of the lifetime of a professor was, believe it or not, zero. In other words, over the course of their careers, more than half of the participants made exactly no changes to the way their contributions were being allocated. Perhaps even more telling, many married participants who were sin-gle when they joined the plan still have their mothers listed as their beneficiaries! Status quo bias is easily exploited. Many years ago American Express wrote Sunstein a cheerful letter telling him that he could receive, for free, three-month subscriptions to five magazines of his choice. Free subscriptions seem like a bargain, even if the magazines rarely get read, so Sunstein happily made his choices. What he didn't realize was that unless he took some action to cancel his subscription, he would continue to receive the magazines, paying for them at the normal rate. For about a decade, he has continued to subscribe to magazines that he hardly ever reads. (He keeps intending to cancel those subscriptions, but somehow never gets around to it. We hope to get around to discussing procrastination in the next chapter.) One of the causes of status quo bias is a lack of attention. Many people adopt what we will call the "yeah, whatever" heuristic. A good illustration is the carryover effect in television viewing. Network executives spend a lot of time working on scheduling because they know that a viewer who starts the evening on nbc tends to stay there. Since remote controls have been pervasive in this country for decades, the actual "switching" costs in this context are literally one thumb press. But when one show ends and the next one comes on, a surprisingly high number of viewers (implicitly) say, "yeah, whatever" and keep watching. Nor is Sunstein the only victim of automatic renewal of magazine subscriptions. Those who are in charge of circulation know that when renewal is automatic, and when people have to make a phone call to cancel, the likelihood of renewal is much higher than it is when people have to indicate that they actually want to continue to receive the magazine. The combination of loss aversion with mindless choosing implies that if an option is designated as the "default," it will attract a large market share. Default options thus act as powerful nudges. In many contexts defaults have some extra nudging power because consumers may feel, rightly or wrongly, that default options come with an implicit endorsement from the default setter, be it the employer, government, or TV scheduler. For this and other reasons, setting the best possible defaults will be a theme we explore often in the course of this book.

Framing Suppose that you are suffering from serious heart disease and that your doctor proposes a grueling operation. You're understandably curious about the odds. The doctor says, "Of one hundred patients who have this operation, ninety are alive after five years." What will you do? If we fill in the facts in a certain way, the doctor's statement will be pretty comforting, and you'll probably have the operation. But suppose the doctor frames his answer in a somewhat different way. Suppose that he says, "Of one hundred patients who have this operation, ten are dead after five years." If you're like most people, the doctor's statement will sound pretty alarming, and you might not have the operation. The Automatic System thinks: "A significant number of people are dead, and I might be one of them!" In numerous experiments, people react very differently to the information that "ninety of one hundred are alive" than to the information that "ten of one hundred are dead"—even though the content of the two statements is exactly the same. Even experts are subject to framing effects. When doctors are told that "ninety of one hundred are alive," they are more likely to recommend the operation than if told that "ten of one hundred are dead."14 Framing matters in many domains. When credit cards started to become popular forms of payment in the 1970s, some retail merchants wanted to charge different prices to their cash and credit card customers. (Credit card companies typically charge retailers 1 percent of each sale.) To prevent this, credit card companies adopted rules that forbade their retailers from charging different prices to cash and credit customers. However, when a bill was introduced in Congress to outlaw such rules, the credit card lobby turned its attention to language. Its preference was that if a company charged different prices to cash and credit customers, the credit price should be considered the "normal" (default) price and the cash price a discount—rather than the alternative of making the cash price the usual price and charging a surcharge to credit card customers. The credit card companies had a good intuitive understanding of what psychologists would come to call "framing." The idea is that choices depend, in part, on the way in which problems are stated. The point matters a great deal for public policy. Energy conservation is now receiving a lot of attention, so consider the following information campaigns: (a) If you use energy conservation methods, you will save $350 per year; (b) If you do not use energy conservation methods, you will lose $350 per year. It turns out that information campaign (b), framed in terms of losses, is far more effective than information campaign (a). If the government wants to encourage energy conservation, option (b) is a stronger nudge. Framing works because people tend to be somewhat mindless, passive decision makers. Their Reflective System does not do the work that would be required to check and see whether reframing the questions would produce a different answer.

One reason they don't do this is that they wouldn't know what to make of the contradiction. This implies that frames are powerful nudges, and must be selected with caution. So What? Our goal in this chapter has been to offer a brief glimpse at human fallibility. The picture that emerges is one of busy people trying to cope in a complex world in which they cannot afford to think deeply about every choice they have to make. People adopt sensible rules of thumb that sometimes lead them astray. Because they are busy and have limited attention, they accept questions as posed rather than trying to determine whether their answers would vary under alternative formulations. The bottom line, from our point of view, is that people are, shall we say, nudge-able. Their choices, even in life's most important decisions, are influenced in ways that would not be anticipated in a standard economic framework. Here is one final example to illustrate. One of the most scenic urban thoroughfares in the world is Chicago's Lake Shore Drive, which hugs the Lake Michigan coastline that is the city's eastern boundary. The drive offers stunning views of Chicago's magnificent skyline. There is one stretch of this road that puts drivers through a series of S curves. These curves are dangerous. Many drivers fail to take heed of the reduced speed limit (25 mph) and wipe out. Recently, the city has employed a new way of encouraging drivers to slow down. At the beginning of the dangerous curve, drivers encounter a sign painted on the road warning of the lower speed limit, and then a series of white stripes painted onto the road. The stripes do not provide much if any tactile information (they are not speed bumps) but rather just send a visual signal to drivers. When the stripes first appear, they are evenly spaced, but as drivers reach the most dangerous portion of the curve, the stripes get closer together, giving the sensation that driving speed is increasing.One's natural instinct is to slow down. When we drive on this familiar stretch of road, we find that those lines are speaking to us, gently urging us to touch the brake before the apex of the curve. We have been nudged.

2

RESISTING TEMPTATION

Temptation Many years ago, Thaler was hosting dinner for some guests (other then-young economists) and put out a large bowl of cashew nuts to nibble on with the first bottle of wine. Within a few minutes it became clear that the bowl of nuts was going to be consumed in its entirety, and that the guests might lack sufficient appetite to enjoy all the food that was to follow. Leaping into action, Thaler grabbed the bowl of nuts, and (while sneaking a few more nuts for himself) removed the bowl to the kitchen, where it was put out of sight. When he returned, the guests thanked him for removing the nuts. The conversation immediately turned to the theoretical question of how they could possibly be happy about the fact that there was no longer a bowl of nuts in front of them. (You can now see the wisdom of the rule of thumb mentioned in Chapter 1 about a cap on the proportion of economists among attendees at a dinner party.) In economics (and in ordinary life), a basic principle is that you can never be made worse off by having more options, because you can always turn them down. Before Thaler removed the nuts the group had the choice of whether to eat the nuts or not—now they didn't. In the land of Econs, it is against the law to be happy about this! To help us understand this example, consider how the preferences of the group seemed to evolve over time. At 7:15, just before Thaler removed the nuts, the dinner guests had three options: eat a few nuts; eat all the nuts; and eat no more nuts. Their first choice would be to eat just a few more nuts, followed by eating no more nuts. The worst option was finishing the bowl, since that would ruin dinner. But by 7:30, had the nuts remained on the table, the group would have finished the bowl, thereby reaching their least favorite option. Why would the group change its mind in the space of just fifteen minutes? Or do we really want to say that the group has changed its mind? In the language of economics, the group is said to display behavior that is dynamically inconsistent. Initially people prefer A to B, but they later choose B over A. We can see dynamic inconsistency in many places. On Saturday morning people might say that they prefer exercising to watching television, but once the afternoon comes, they are on the couch at home watching the football game. How can such behavior be understood? Two factors must be introduced in order to understand the cashew phenomenon: temptation and mindlessness. Human beings have been aware of the concept of temptation at least since the time of Adam and Eve, but for purposes of understanding the value of nudges, that concept needs elaboration. What does it mean for something to be "tempting"? As with Supreme Court Justice Potter Stewart's "I know it when I see it" adage about pornography, temptation is easier to recognize than to define. Our preferred definition requires recognizing that people's state of arousal varies over time. To simplify things we will consider just the two end points: hot and cold. When Sally is very hungry and appetizing aromas are emanating from the kitchen, we can say she is in a hot state. When Sally is thinking abstractly on Tuesday about the right number of cashews she should consume before dinner on Saturday, she is in a cold state. We will call something "tempting" if we consume more of it when hot than when cold. None of this means that decisions made in a cold state are always better. For example, sometimes we have to be in a hot state to overcome our fears about trying new things. Sometimes dessert really is delicious, and we do best to go for it. Sometimes it is best to fall in love. But it is clear that when we are in a hot state, we can often get into a lot of trouble. Most people realize that temptation exists, and they take steps to overcome it. The classic example is that of Ulysses, who faced the peril of the Sirens and their irresistible songs. While in a cold state, Ulysses instructed his crew to fill their ears with wax so that they would not be tempted by the music. He also asked the crew to tie him to the mast so that he could listen for himself but be restrained from submitting to the temptation to steer the ship closer when the music put him into a hot state. Ulysses successfully solved his problem. For most of us, however, selfcontrol issues arise because we underestimate the effect of arousal. This is something the behavioral economist George Loewenstein (1996) calls the "hot-cold empathy gap." When in a cold state, we do not appreciate how much our desires and our behavior will be altered when we are "under the influence" of arousal. As a result, our behavior reflects a certain naïveté about the effects that context can have on choice. Tom is on a diet and agrees to go out on a business dinner, thinking that he will be able to limit himself to one glass of wine and no dessert. But the host orders a second bottle of wine and the waiter brings by the dessert cart, and all bets are off. Marilyn thinks that she can go into a department store when they are having a big sale and just see whether they have something on sale that she really needs. She ends up with shoes that hurt (but were 70 percent off). Robert thinks he will engage only in safe sex, but then must make all the crucial decisions while aroused. Similar problems affect those who have problems with smoking, alcohol, a failure to exercise, excessive borrowing, and insufficient savings. Self-control problems can be illuminated by thinking about an individual as containing two semiautonomous selves, a far-sighted "Planner" and a myopic "Doer." You can think of the Planner as speaking for your Reflective System, or the Mr. Spock lurking within you, and the Doer as heavily influenced by the Automatic System, or everyone's Homer Simpson. The Planner is trying to promote your long-term welfare but must cope with the feelings, mischief, and strong will of the Doer, who is exposed to the temptations that come with arousal. Recent research in neuroeconomics (yes, there really is such a field) has found evidence consistent with this two-system conception of self-control. Some parts of the brain get tempted, and other parts are prepared to enable us to resist temptation by assessing how we should react to the temptation.1 Sometimes the two parts of the brain can be in severe conflict—a kind of battle that one or the other is bound to lose.Mindless Choosing The cashew problem is not only one of temptation. It also involves the type of mindless behavior we discussed in the context of inertia. In many situations, people put themselves into an "automatic pilot" mode, in which they are not actively paying attention to the task at hand. (The Automatic System is very comfortable that way.) On a Saturday morning when we set out to run an errand, we can easily find ourselves driving our usual route to work—until we realize we are headed in the opposite direction from our intended destination, the grocery store. On a Sunday morning, we follow our ordinary routine with coffee and the newspaper—until we realize that we had arranged to meet a friend for brunch an hour earlier. Eating turns out to be one of the most mindless activities we do. Many of us simply eat whatever is put in front of us. That is why even massive bowls of cashews are likely to be consumed completely, regardless of the quality of the food that is soon to be arriving. The same is true of popcorn—even stale popcorn. A few years ago, Brian Wansink and his colleagues ran an experiment in a

Chicago movie theater in which moviegoers found themselves with a free bucket of stale popcorn.2 (It had been popped five days earlier and stored so as to ensure that it would actually squeak when eaten.) People were not specifically informed of its staleness, but they didn't like the popcorn. As one moviegoer said, "It was like eating Styrofoam packing peanuts." In the experiment, half of the moviegoers received a big bucket of popcorn and half received a medium-sized bucket. On average, recipients of the big bucket ate about 53 percent more popcorn—even though they didn't really like it. After the movie, Wansink asked the recipients of the big bucket whether they might have eaten more because of the size of their bucket. Most denied the possibility, saying, "Things like that don't trick me." But they were wrong. The same is true of soup. In another Wansink (2006) masterpiece, people sat down to a large bowl of Campbell's tomato soup and were told to eat as much as they wanted. Unbeknownst to them, the soup bowls were designed to refill themselves (with empty bottoms connected to machinery beneath the table). No matter how much soup subjects ate, the bowl never emptied. Many people just kept eating, not paying attention to the fact that they were really eating a great deal of soup, until the experiment was (mercifully) ended. Large plates and large packages mean more eating; they are a form of choice architecture, and they work as major nudges. (Hint: if you would like to lose weight, get smaller plates, buy little packages of what you like, and don't keep tempting food in the refrigerator.) When self-control problems and mindless choosing are combined, the result is a series of bad outcomes for real people. Millions of Americans still smoke in spite of the evidence that smoking has terrible health consequences, and, significantly, the overwhelming majority of smokers say that they would like to quit. Nearly two-thirds of Americans are overweight or obese. Many people never get around to joining their company's retirement savings plan, even when it is heavily subsidized. Together, these facts suggest that significant numbers of people could benefit from a nudge. Self-Control Strategies Since people are at least partly aware of their weaknesses, they take steps to engage outside help. We make lists to help us remember what to buy at the grocery store. We buy an alarm clock to help us get up in the morning. We ask friends to stop us from having dessert or to fortify our efforts to quit smoking. In these cases, our Planners are taking steps to control the actions of our Doers, often by trying to change the incentives that Doers face. Unfortunately, Doers are often difficult to rein in (think of controlling Homer), and they can foil the best efforts of Planners. Consider the mundane but revealing example of the alarm clock. The optimistic Planner sets the alarm for 6:15 a.m., hoping for a full day of work, but the sleepy Doer turns off the alarm and goes back to sleep until 9:00. This can lead to fierce battles between the Planner and the Doer. Some Planners put the alarm clock on the other side of the room, so the Doer at least has to get up to turn it off, but if the Doer crawls back into bed, all is lost. Fortunately, enterprising firms sometimes offer to help the Planner out. Consider the alarm clock "Clocky," pictured in Figure 2.1. Clocky is the "alarm clock that runs away and hides if you don't get out of bed." With Clocky, the Planner sets the number of snooze minutes the Doer will be permitted in the morning. When that number runs out, the clock jumps off the night stand and moves around the room making annoying sounds.

The only way to turn the damn thing off is to get out of bed and find it. By that time, even a groggy Doer is awake. Planners have a number of available strategies, such as Clocky, to control recalcitrant Doers, but they can sometimes use some help from outsiders. We will be exploring how private and public institutions can provide that help. In daily life, one strategy involves informal bets. Thaler once helped a young colleague by using this strategy. The colleague (let's call him David) had been hired as a new faculty member with the expectation that he would complete the requirements for his Ph.D. before he arrived, or at worst within his first year as a faculty member. David had lots of incentives to finish his thesis, including a strong financial incentive: until he graduated the university treated him as an "instructor" rather than an assistant professor and did not make its normal contributions to his retirement plan, which amounted to 10 percent of his salary (thousands of dollars a year). David's inner Planner knew that he needed to stop procrastinating and get his thesis done, but his Doer was involved in many other more exciting projects and always put off the drudgery of writing up the thesis. (Thinking about new ideas is usually more fun than writing up old ones.) That is when Thaler intervened by offering David the following deal. David would write Thaler a series of checks for $100, payable on the first day of each of the next few months. Thaler would cash each check if David did not put a copy of a new chapter of the thesis under his door by midnight of the corresponding month. Furthermore, Thaler promised to use the money to have a party to which David would not be invited. David completed his thesis on schedule four months later, never having missed a deadline (though most chapters were completed within mere minutes of being due). It is instructive that this incentive scheme worked even though David's monetary incentive from the university was greater than $100 a month, just from the retirement contribution alone. The scheme worked because the pain of having Thaler cash the check and consume some good wine without him was more salient than the rather abstract and pallid forgone contribution to his retirement savings plan. Many of Thaler's friends have threatened to go into business competing with him on this incentive plan, though Thaler points out that in order to go into this business, you have to be known as a big enough jerk actually to cash the check. Sometimes friends can adopt such betting strategies together. John Romalis and Dean Karlan, two economists, adopted an ingenious arrangement for weight loss. When John and Dean were in graduate school in economics, they noticed that they were putting on weight, especially during the period when they were on the job market and being wined and dined by potential employers. They made a pact. Each agreed to lose thirty pounds over a period of nine months. If either failed, he had to pay the other $10,000. The bet was a big success; both met their target. They then turned to the more difficult problem of keeping the weight off. The rules they adopted were that on one day's notice, either one could call for a weigh-in. If either was found to be over the target weight, he would have to pay the other an agreed sum. In four years, there were several weigh-ins, and only once was either one over target (the resulting fine was paid in full immediately). Notice that as in the case of David's thesis bet, Dean and John were acknowledging that without the bet to encourage them, they would have eaten too much, even though they still would have wanted to lose the weight. More formal versions of these strategies are easy to imagine. In Chapter 16 we will encounter the Web site Stickk.com (of which Karlan is a cofounder), which gives people a method by which their Planners can constrain their Doers. In some situations, people may even want the government to help them deal with their self-control problems. In extreme cases, governments might ban some items (such as heroin use, prostitution, and drunken driving). Such bans can be seen as pure rather than libertarian paternalism, though third-party interests are also at stake. In other cases, individuals may prefer a less intrusive role for the government. For example, smokers might benefit from cigarette taxes, which discourage consumption without forbidding it.3 Also, some states have attempted to help gamblers by creating a mechanism by which they can put themselves on a list of people who are banned from casinos (again see Chapter 16 for details). Since no one is required to sign up, and since a refusal to do so is close to costless, this approach really can be counted as libertarian as we understand the term. One interesting example of a government-imposed self-control strategy is daylight saving time (or summer time, as it is called in many parts of the world). Surveys reveal that most people think that daylight saving time is a great idea, primarily because they enjoy the "extra" hour of daylight during the evening. Of course, the number of daylight hours on a given day is fixed, and setting the clocks ahead one hour does nothing to increase the amount of daylight. The simple change of the labels on the hours of the day, calling "six o'clock" by the name "seven o'clock," nudges us all into waking up an hour earlier. Along with having more time to enjoy an evening softball game, we end up saving energy too. Historical note: the idea was first suggested by Benjamin Franklin during his tenure as an American delegate in Paris. A well-known skinflint, Franklin calculated that thousands of pounds of candle wax could be saved with his idea. However, the idea did not catch on until World War I.

In many cases, markets provide self-control services, and government is not needed at all. Companies can make a lot of money by strengthening Planners in their battle with Doers, often doing well by doing good. An interesting example is a distinctive financial services institution that used to be quite popular: the Christmas savings club. Here is how a Christmas club typically works. In November (around Thanksgiving) a customer opens an account at her local bank and commits herself to depositing a given amount (say $10) each week for the next year. Funds cannot be withdrawn until a year later, when the total amount is redeemed, just in time for the Christmas shopping season. The usual interest rate on these accounts is close to zero. Think about the Christmas club in economic terms. This is an account with no liquidity (you can't take your money out for a year), high transaction costs (you have to make deposits every week), and a near-zero rate of return. It is an easy homework exercise in an economics class to prove that such an institution cannot exist. Yet for many years Christmas clubs were widely used, with billions of dollars in investments. If we realize that we are dealing with Humans rather than Econs, it is not hard to explain why the clubs flourished. Households lacking enough money for Christmas giving would resolve to solve the problem next year by joining a Christmas club. The inconvenience of making the deposits and the loss of money paid in interest would be small prices to pay in return for the assurance of having enough money to buy gifts. And think back to Ulysses, tying himself to the mast—the fact that money could not be withdrawn was a plus, not a minus. The absence of liquidity was precisely the point. Christmas clubs are in many ways an adult version of a child's piggy bank, designed to make it easier to put money in than to take money out. The fact that it is hard to withdraw money is entirely the point of the device. While Christmas clubs still exist, they have been made unnecessary for most households by the advent of credit cards.* Since Christmas shopping can now be financed, households no longer find it necessary to save up in advance. This is not to say, of course, that the new regime is in all respects better. Saving at a zero percent interest rate with no opportunity to withdraw the funds may seem dumb, and it is clearly worse than just depositing the money into an interest-bearing account, but earning a zero interest rate may well be preferable to paying 18 percent or more on credit card debt. The market battle between credit cards and Christmas clubs is a good illustration of a more general point, one to which we will return. Markets provide strong incentives for firms to cater to the demands of consumers, and firms will compete to meet those demands, whether or not those demands represent the wisest choices. One firm might devise a clever selfcontrol device such as a Christmas club, but that firm cannot prevent another firm from offering to lend people money in anticipation of the receipts of those funds. Credit cards and Christmas clubs compete, and indeed both are offered by the same institutions—banks. While competition does drive down prices, it does not always lead to an outcome that is best for consumers. Even when we're on our way to making good choices, competitive markets find ways to get us to overcome our last shred of resistance to bad ones. At O'Hare Airport in Chicago, two food vendors compete across the aisle from each other. One sells fruit, yogurt, and other healthy foods. The other sells Cinnabons, sinful cinnamon buns that have a whopping 730 calories and 24 grams of fat. Your Planner may have set the course for the yogurt and fruit stand, but the Cinnabon outlet blasts the aromas from their ovens directly into the walkway in front of the store. Care to guess which of the two stores always has the longer line? Mental Accounting Alarm clocks and Christmas clubs are external devices people use to solve their self-control problems. Another way to approach these problems is to adopt internal control systems, otherwise known as mental accounting. Mental accounting is the system (sometimes implicit) that households use to evaluate, regulate, and process their home budget. Almost all of us use mental accounts, even if we're not aware that we're doing so. The concept is beautifully illustrated by an exchange between the actors Gene Hackman and Dustin Hoffman in one of those extra features offered on dvds. Hackman and Hoffman were friends back in their starving artist days, and Hackman tells the story of visiting Hoffman's apartment and having his host ask him for a loan. Hackman agreed to the loan, but then they went into Hoffman's kitchen, where several mason jars were lined up on the counter, each containing money. One jar was labeled "rent," another "utilities," and so forth. Hackman asked why, if Hoffman had so much money in jars, he could possibly need a loan, whereupon Hoffman pointed to the food jar, which was empty. According to economic theory (and simple logic), money is "fungible," meaning that it doesn't come with labels. Twenty dollars in the rent jar can buy just as much food as the same amount in the food jar. But households adopt mental accounting schemes that violate fungibility for the same reasons that organizations do: to control spending. Most organizations have budgets for various activities, and anyone who has ever worked in such an organization has experienced the frustration of not being able to make an important purchase because the relevant account is already depleted. The fact that there is unspent money in another account is considered no more relevant than the money sitting in the rent jar on Dustin Hoffman's kitchen counter. At the household level, violations of fungibility are everywhere. One of the most creative examples of mental accounting was invented by a finance professor we know. At the beginning of each year, he designates a certain amount of money (say $2,000) as his intended gift to the United Way charity. Then if anything bad happens to him during the year—a parking ticket, for example—he mentally deducts the fine against the United Way gift. This provides him "insurance" against minor financial mishaps.* You can also see mental accounting in action at the casino. Watch a gambler who is lucky enough to win some money early in the evening. You might see him take the money he has won and put it into one pocket and put the money he brought with him to gamble that evening (yet another mental account) into a different pocket. Gamblers even have a term for this. The money that has recently been won is called "house money" because in gambling parlance the casino is referred to as the house. Betting some of the money that you have just won is referred to as "gambling with the house's money," as if it were, somehow, different from some other kind of money. Experimental evidence reveals that people are more willing to gamble with money that they consider house money.4 This same mentality affects people who never gamble. When investments pay off, people are willing to take big chances with their "winnings." For example, mental accounting contributed to the large increase in stock prices in the 1990s, as many people took on more and more risk with the justification that they were playing only with their gains from the past few years. Similarly, people are far more likely to splurge impulsively on a big luxury purchase when they receive an unexpected windfall than with savings that they have accumulated over time, even if those savings are fully available to be spent. Mental accounting matters precisely because the accounts are treated as nonfungible. True, the mason jars used by Dustin Hoffman (and his parents' generation) have largely disappeared. But many households continue to designate accounts for various uses: children's education, vacations, retirement, and so forth. In many cases these are literally different accounts, as opposed to entries in a ledger. The sanctity of these accounts can lead to seemingly bizarre behavior, such as simultaneously borrowing and lending at very different rates. David Gross and Nick Souleles (2002) found that the typical household in their sample had more than $5,000 in liquid assets (typically in savings accounts earning less than 5 percent a year) and nearly $3,000 in credit card balances, carrying a typical interest rate of 18 percent or more. Using the money from the savings account to pay off the credit card debt amounts to what economists call an arbitrage opportunity— buying low and selling high—but the vast majority of households fail to take advantage. Just as with Christmas clubs, though, this behavior might not be as stupid as it looks. Many of these households have borrowed up to the limits that their credit cards set. They may realize that if they paid off the credit card debt from the savings account, they would soon run up the cards to their limits once again. (And credit card companies, fully aware of this, are often more than willing to extend more credit to those who have reached the limit, as long as they aren't yet falling behind on interest payments.) Keeping the money in the separate accounts is thus another costly selfcontrol strategy, just like the Christmas club. Of course, many people do not suffer from an inability to save. Some people actually have trouble spending. If their problem is extreme, we call such people misers, but even regular folks can find that they don't give themselves enough treats. We have a friend named Dennis who has adopted a clever mental accounting strategy to deal with this problem. When Dennis turned sixty-five, he started collecting Social Security payments, although both he and his wife continue to work full-time. Since he has been a good saver over the years (in part because his employer has a mandatory and generous retirement plan), Dennis wanted to be sure he would do the things he enjoys (especially trips to Paris with lots of eating) now while he is still healthy, and not be put off by the expense. So he opened a special savings account for his Social Security checks and has designated the money in this account as a "fun account." A fancy new bike or a case of good wine would be acceptable purchases from this account, but a repair to the roof would certainly not. For each of us, using mental accounts can be extremely valuable. They make life both more fun and more secure. Many of us could benefit from a near-sacrosanct "rainy day" account and from a freely available "entertainment and fun" account. Understanding mental accounts would also improve public policy. As we will see, if we want to encourage savings, it will be important to direct the increased savings into a mental (or real) account where spending it will not be too big a temptation.

3

FOLLOWING THE HERD

The Reverend Jim Jones was the founder and leader of the People's Temple. In 1978 Jones, facing charges of tax evasion, moved most of his one thousand followers from San Francisco to a small settlement in Guyana, which he named Jonestown. Facing a federal investigation for reported acts of child abuse and torture, Jones decided that his followers should poison their children and then themselves. They prepared vats of poison. A few people resisted; a few others shouted out their protest, but they were silenced. Following Jones's orders, and the social pressures imposed by one another, mothers and fathers duly poisoned their children. Then they poisoned themselves. Their bodies were found arm in arm, lying together.1 Econs (and some economists we know) are pretty unsociable creatures. They communicate with others if they can gain something from the encounter, they care about their reputations, and they will learn from others if actual information can be obtained, but Econs are not followers of fashion. Their hemlines would not go up and down except for practical reasons, and ties, if they existed at all in a world of Econs, would not grow narrower and wider simply as a matter of style. (By the way, ties were originally used as napkins; they actually had a function.) Humans, on the other hand, are frequently nudged by other Humans. Sometimes massive social changes, in markets and politics alike, start with a small social nudge. Humans are not exactly lemmings, but they are easily influenced by the statements and deeds of others. (Again by the way, lemmings do not really commit mass suicide by following one another into the ocean. Our widely shared and somewhat defamatory beliefs about lemmings are based on an all-too-human urban legend—that is, people believe this because they are following other people. By contrast, the tale of mass suicide at Jonestown is no legend.) If you see a movie scene in which people are smiling, you are more likely to smile yourself (whether or not the movie is funny); yawns are contagious, too. Conventional wisdom has it that if two people live together for a long time, they start to look like each other. This bit of folk wisdom turns out to be true. (For the curious: they grow to look alike partly because of nutrition—shared diets and eating habits—but much of the effect is simple imitation of facial expressions.) In fact couples who end up looking alike also tend to be happier! In this chapter, we try to understand how and why social influences work. An understanding of those influences is important in our context for two reasons. First, most people learn from others. This is usually good, of course. Learning from others is how individuals and societies develop. But many of our biggest misconceptions also come from others. When social influences have caused people to have false or biased beliefs, then some nudging may help. The second reason why this topic is important for our purposes is that one of the most effective ways to nudge (for good or evil) is via social influence. In Jonestown, that influence was so strong that an entire population committed suicide. But social influences have also created miracles, large and small. In many cities, including ours, dog owners now carry plastic bags when they walk their dogs, and strolling through the park has become much more pleasant as a result. This has happened even though the risk of being fined for unclean dog walking is essentially zero. Choice architects need to know how to encourage other socially beneficial behavior, and also how to discourage events like the one that occurred in Jonestown. Social influences come in two basic categories. The first involves information. If many people do something or think something, their actions and their thoughts convey information about what might be best for you to do or think. The second involves peer pressure. If you care about what other people think about you (perhaps in the mistaken belief that they are paying some attention to what you are doing—see below), then you might go along with the crowd to avoid their wrath or curry their favor.

For a quick glance at the power of social nudges, consider just a few research findings: 1. Teenage girls who see that other teenagers are having children are more likely to become pregnant themselves.* 2. Obesity is contagious. If your best friends get fat, your risk of gaining weight goes up. 3. Broadcasters mimic one another, producing otherwise inexplicable fads in programming. (Think reality television, American Idol and its siblings, game shows that come and go, the rise and fall and rise of science fiction, and so forth.) 4. The academic effort of college students is influenced by their peers, so much so that the random assignments of first-year students to dormitories or roommates can have big consequences for their grades and hence on their future prospects. (Maybe parents should worry less about which college their kids go to and more about which roommate they get.) 5. Federal judges on three-judge panels are affected by the votes of their colleagues. The typical Republican appointee shows pretty liberal voting patterns when sitting with two Democratic appointees, and the typical Democratic appointee shows pretty conservative voting patterns when sitting with two Republican appointees. Both sets of appointees show far more moderate voting patterns when they are sitting with at least one judge appointed by a president of the opposing political party.2 The bottom line is that Humans are easily nudged by other Humans. Why? One reason is that we like to conform. Doing What Others Do Imagine that you find yourself in a group of six people, engaged in a test of visual perception. You are given a ridiculously simple task. You are FOLLOWING THE HERD 55 *For this and all the other examples, we leave out the implied phrase "holding everything else constant." So what we mean here is that controlling for other risk factors that predict teenage pregnancy, girls are more likely to get pregnant if they see other girls doing so.

supposed to match a particular line, shown on a large white card, to the one of three comparison lines, projected onto a screen, that is identical to it in length. In the first three rounds of this test, everything proceeds smoothly and easily. People make their matches aloud, in sequence, and everyone agrees with everyone else. But on the fourth round, something odd happens. The five other people in the group announce their matches before you—and every one makes an obvious error. It is now time for you to make your announcement. What will you do? If you are like most people, you think it is easy to predict your behavior in this task: You will say exactly what you think. You'll call it as you see it. You are independent-minded and so you will tell the truth. But if you are a Human, and you really participated in the experiment, you might well follow those who preceded you, and say what they say, thus defying the evidence of your own senses. In the 1950s Solomon Asch (1995), a brilliant social psychologist, conducted a series of experiments in just this vein. When asked to decide on their own, without seeing judgments from others, people almost never erred, since the test was easy. But when everyone else gave an incorrect answer, people erred more than one-third of the time. Indeed, in a series of twelve questions, nearly three-quarters of people went along with the group at least once, defying the evidence of their own senses. Notice that in Asch's experiment, people were responding to the decisions of strangers, whom they would probably never see again. They had no particular reason to want those strangers to like them. Asch's findings seem to capture something universal about humanity. Conformity experiments have been replicated and extended in more than 130 experiments from seventeen countries, including Zaire, Germany, France, Japan, Norway, Lebanon, and Kuwait (Sunstein, 2003). The overall pattern of errors—with people conforming between 20 and 40 percent of the time—does not show huge differences across nations. And though 20 to 40 percent of the time might not seem large, remember that this task was very simple. It is almost as if people can be nudged into identifying a picture of a dog as a cat as long as other people before them have done so. Why, exactly, do people sometimes ignore the evidence of their own senses? We have already sketched the two answers. The first involves the in formation conveyed by people's answers; the second involves peer pressure and the desire not to face the disapproval of the group. In Asch's own studies, several of the conformists said, in private interviews, that their initial perceptions must have been wrong. If everyone in the room accepts a certain proposition, or sees things in a certain way, you might conclude that they are probably right. Remarkably, recent brain-imaging work has suggested that when people conform in Asch-like settings, they actually see the situation as everyone else does.3 On the other hand, social scientists generally find less conformity, in the same basic circumstances as Asch's experiments, when people are asked to give anonymous answers. People become more likely to conform when they know that other people will see what they have to say. Sometimes people will go along with the group even when they think, or know, that everyone else has blundered. Unanimous groups are able to provide the strongest nudges—even when the question is an easy one, and people ought to know that everyone else is wrong. Asch's experiments involved evaluations with pretty obvious answers. Most of the time, it isn't hard to assess the length of lines. What if the task is made a bit more difficult? The question is especially important for our purposes, because we are particularly interested in how people are influenced, or can be influenced, in dealing with problems that are both hard and unfamiliar. Some key studies were undertaken in the 1930s by the psychologist Muzafer Sherif (1937). In Sherif's experiment, people were placed in a dark room, and a small pinpoint of light was positioned at some distance in front of them. The light was actually stationary, but because of a perceptual illusion called the autokinetic effect, it appeared to move. On each of several trials, Sherif asked people to estimate the distance that the light had moved. When polled individually, subjects did not agree with one another, and their answers varied significantly from one trial to another. This is not surprising; because the light did not move, any judgment about distance was a stab in the literal dark. But Sherif found big conformity effects when people were asked to act in small groups and to make their estimates in public. Here the individual judgments converged and a group norm, establishing the consensus distance, quickly developed. Over time, the norm remained stable within particular groups, thus leading to a situation in which different groups made, and were strongly committed to, quite different judgments. There is an important clue here about how seemingly similar groups, cities, and even nations can converge on very different beliefs and actions simply because of modest and even arbitrary variations in starting points. Sherif also tried a nudge. In some experiments, he added a confederate—his own ally, unbeknownst to the people in the study. When he did that, something else happened. If the confederate spoke confidently and firmly, his judgment had a strong influence on the group's assessment. If the confederate's estimate was much higher than those initially made by others, the group's judgment would be inflated; if the confederate's estimate was very low, the group's estimate would fall. A little nudge, if it was expressed confidently, could have major consequences for the group's conclusion. The clear lesson here is that consistent and unwavering people, in the private or public sector, can move groups and practices in their preferred direction. More remarkable still, the group's judgments became thoroughly internalized, so that people would adhere to them even when reporting on their own—indeed even a year later, and even when participating in new groups whose members offered different judgments. Significantly, the initial judgments were also found to have effects across "generations." Even when enough fresh subjects were introduced and others retired so that all the participants were new to the situation, the original group judgment tended to stick, although the person who was originally responsible for it had been long gone.4 In a series of experiments, people using Sherif's basic method have shown that an arbitrary "tradition," in the form of some judgment about the distance, can become entrenched over time, so that many people follow it notwithstanding its original arbitrariness.5 We can see here why many groups fall prey to what is known as "collective conservatism": the tendency of groups to stick to established patterns even as new needs arise. Once a practice (like wearing ties) has become established, it is likely to be perpetuated, even if there is no particular basis for it. Sometimes a tradition can last for a long time, and receive support or at least acquiescence from large numbers of people, even though it was originally the product of a small nudge from a few people or perhaps even one. Of course, a group will shift if it can be shown that the practice is causing serious problems. But if there is uncertainty on that question, people might well continue doing what they have always done. An important problem here is "pluralistic ignorance"—that is, ignorance, on the part of all or most, about what other people think. We may follow a practice or a tradition not because we like it, or even think it defensible, but merely because we think that most other people like it. Many social practices persist for this reason, and a small shock, or nudge, can dislodge them.6 A dramatic example is communism in the former Soviet bloc, which lasted in part because people were unaware how many people despised the regime. Dramatic but less world-historical changes, rejecting long-standing practices, can often be produced by a nudge that starts a kind of bandwagon effect. Additional experiments, growing out of Asch's basic method, find large conformity effects for judgments of many different kinds.7 Consider the following finding. People were asked, "Which one of the following do you feel is the most important problem facing our country today?" Five alternatives were offered: economic recession, educational facilities, subversive activities, mental health, and crime and corruption. Asked privately, a mere 12 percent chose subversive activities. But when exposed to an apparent group consensus unanimously selecting that option, 48 percent of people made the same choice! In a similar finding, people were asked to consider this statement: "Free speech being a privilege rather than a right, it is proper for a society to suspend free speech when it feels threatened." Asked this question individually, only 19 percent of the control group agreed, but confronted with the shared opinion of only four others, 58 percent of people agreed. These results are closely connected with one of Asch's underlying interests, which was to understand how Nazism had been possible. Asch believed that conformity could produce a very persistent nudge, ultimately generating behavior (such as the events in Jonestown) that might seem unthinkable. Whether or not Asch's work provides an adequate account of the rise of fascism, or the events in Jonestown, there is no question that social pressures nudge people to accept some pretty odd conclusions—and those conclusions might well affect their behavior. An obvious question is whether choice architects can exploit this fact to move people in better directions. Suppose, for example, that a city is trying to encourage people to exercise more, so as to improve their health. If many people are exercising, the city might be able to produce significant changes simply by mentioning that fact. A few influential people, offering strong signals about appropriate behavior, can have a similar effect. Consider Texas's imaginative and stunningly successful effort to reduce littering on its highways.8 Texas officials were enormously frustrated by the failure of their well-funded and highly publicized advertising campaigns, which attempted to convince people that it was their civic duty to stop littering. Many of the litterers were men between the ages of eighteen and twenty-four, who were not exactly impressed by the idea that a bureaucratic elite wanted them to change their behavior. Public officials decided that they needed "a tough-talking slogan that would also address the unique spirit of Texas pride." Explicitly targeting the unresponsive audience, the state enlisted popular Dallas Cowboys football players to participate in television ads in which they collected litter, smashed beer cans in their bare hands, and growled, "Don't mess with Texas!" Other spots included popular singers, such as Willie Nelson. People can now get all kinds of "Don't Mess with Texas" products, from decals to shirts to coffee mugs. One popular decal offers patriotic colors, reflecting both the U.S. flag, and—perhaps more important—the Texas flag (Figure 3.1)! About 95 percent of Texans now know this slogan, and in 2006 "Don't Mess with Texas" was voted America's favorite slogan by a landslide and was honored with a parade down New York City's Madison Avenue. (We are not making this up. Only in America, to be sure.) More to the point: Within the first year of the campaign, litter in the state had been reduced by a remarkable 29 percent. In its first six years, there was a 72 percent reduction in visible roadside litter. All this happened not through mandates, threats, or coercion but through a creative nudge. The Spotlight Effect One reason why people expend so much effort conforming to social norms and fashions is that they think that others are closely paying attention to what they are doing. If you wear a suit to a social event where everyone else has gone casual, you feel like everyone is looking at you funny and wondering why you are such a geek. If you are subject to such fears, here is a possibly comforting thought: they aren't really paying as much attention to you as you think. Tom Gilovich and his colleagues have demonstrated that people fall prey to what he calls the "spotlight effect."9 In a typical experiment, Gilovich's team started by doing some research about which entertainer would be most unhip to display on the front of a T-shirt. This research was conducted in the late 1990s, and the winner of this dubious honor was the singer Barry Manilow. When a student arrived for the experiment, he was told to put on a T-shirt with Barry Manilow's picture prominently displayed on the front. The student was then asked to join another group of students who were busy filling out questionnaires. After a minute or so, the experimenter returned, and told the student wearing the T-shirt that he now realized he wanted him to participate in a different study. The student and the experimenter then left the room. At this point the student was asked to guess how many of the other students in the room would be able to identify who was on his T-shirt. The average guess was a bit less then half, 46 percent. In fact, only 21 percent of the group could say who was pictured on his T-shirt.The moral is that people are paying less attention to you than you believe. If you have a stain on your shirt, don't worry, they probably won't notice. But in part because people do think that everyone has their eyes fixed on them, they conform to what they think people expect. Cultural Change, Political Change, and Unpredictability Might culture and politics be affected by conformity? Might companies be able to make money by enlisting conformity? Consider some evidence involving music downloads. Matthew Salganik and his coauthors (2006) created an artificial music market, with 14,341 participants who were visitors to a Web site popular with young people. The participants were given a list of previously unknown songs from unknown bands. They were asked to listen to a brief selection of any songs that interested them, to decide which songs (if any) to download, and to assign a rating to the songs they chose. About half of the participants were asked to make their decisions independently, based on the names of the bands and the songs and their own judgment about the quality of the music. The other half could see how many times each song had been downloaded by other participants. Each participant in this second group was also randomly assigned to one or another of eight possible "worlds," each of which evolved on its own; those in any particular world could see only the downloads in their own world. A key question was whether people would be affected by the choices of others—and whether different music would become popular in the different "worlds." Were people nudged by what other people did? There is not the slightest doubt. In all eight worlds, individuals were far more likely to download songs that had been previously downloaded in significant numbers, and far less likely to download songs that had not been as popular.

Most strikingly, the success of songs was quite unpredictable, and the songs that did well or poorly in the control group, where people did not see other people's judgments, could perform very differently in the "social influence worlds." In those worlds, most songs could become popular or unpopular, with much depending on the choices of the first downloaders. The identical song could be a hit or a failure simply because other people, at the start, were seen to choose to have downloaded it or not.In many domains people are tempted to think, after the fact, that an outcome was entirely predictable, and that the success of a musician, an actor, an author, or a politician was inevitable in light of his of her skills and characteristics. Beware of that temptation. Small interventions and even coincidences, at a key stage, can produce large variations in the outcome. Today's hot singer is probably indistinguishable from dozens and even hundreds of equally talented performers whose names you've never heard. We can go further. Most of today's governors are hard to distinguish from dozens or even hundreds of politicians whose candidacies badly fizzled. The effects of social influences may or may not be deliberately planned by particular people. For a vivid and somewhat hilarious example of how social influences can affect beliefs even if no one plans anything, consider the Seattle Windshield Pitting Epidemic.10 In late March 1954, a group of people in Bellingham, Washington, noticed some tiny holes, or pits, on their windshields. Local police speculated that the pits had resulted from the actions of vandals, using BBs or buckshot. Soon thereafter, a few people in cities south of Bellingham reported similar damage to their windshields. Within two weeks, the apparent work of vandals had gone even farther south, to the point where two thousand cars were reported as damaged— these evidently not the work of vandals. The threat approached Seattle. The Seattle newspapers duly reported the risk in mid-April, and soon thereafter, several reports of windshield pits came to the attention of local police. Before long those reports reached epidemic proportions, leading to intense speculation about what on earth, or elsewhere, could possibly be the cause. Geiger counters found no radioactivity. Some people thought that some odd atmospheric event must have been responsible; others invoked sound waves and a possible shift in the earth's magnetic field; still others pointed to cosmic rays from the sun. By April 16 no fewer than three thousand windshields in the Seattle area were reported to have been "pitted," and Seattle's mayor promptly wrote the governor and President Eisenhower: "What appeared to be a localized outbreak of vandalism in damaged auto windshields and windows in the northern part of Washington State has now spread throughout the Puget Sound area. . . . Urge appropriate federal (and state) agencies be instructed to cooperate with local authorities on emergency basis." In response, the governor created a committee of scientists to investigate this ominous and startling phenomenon. Their conclusion? The damage, such as it was, was probably "the result of normal driving conditions in which small objects strike the windshields of cars." A later investigation, supporting the scientists' conclusion, found that brand new cars lacked pits. The eventual judgment was that the pits "had been there all along, but no one had noticed them until now." (You might have a look at your car right now; if you've had it for a while, there's probably a pit, or two, or more.) The Seattle Windshield Pitting Epidemic was an extreme example of unintentional social nudging, but every day we are influenced by people who are not trying to influence us. Most of us are affected by the eating habits of our eating companions, whatever their intentions. As we have said, obesity is contagious; you're more likely to be overweight if you have a lot of overweight friends. An especially good way to gain weight is to have dinner with other people.11 On average, those who eat with one other person eat about 35 percent more than they do when they are alone; members of a group of four eat about 75 percent more; those in groups of seven or more eat 96 percent more.* We are also greatly influenced by consumption norms within the relevant group. A light eater eats much more in a group of heavy eaters. A heavy eater will show more restraint in a light-eating group. The group average thus exerts a significant influence. But there are gender differences as well. Women often eat less on dates; men tend to eat a lot more, apparently with the belief that women are impressed by a lot of manly eating. (Note to men: they aren't.) So if you want to lose some weight, look for a thin colleague to go to lunch with (and don't finish the food on her plate). If you find yourself nudged by your friends' eating choices, it is unlikely to be because one or another friend decided to nudge you. At the same time, social influences are often used strategically. In particular, advertisers are entirely aware of the power of social influences. Frequently they emphasize that "most people prefer" their own product, or that "growing numbers of people" are switching from another brand, which was yesterday's news, to their own, which represents the future. They try to nudge you by telling you what most people are now doing. Candidates for public office, or political parties, do the same thing; they emphasize that "most people are turning to" their preferred candidates, hoping that the very statement can make itself true. Nothing is worse than a perception that voters are leaving a candidate in droves. Indeed, a perception of that kind helped to account for the Democratic nomination of John Kerry in 2004. When Democrats shifted from Howard Dean to John Kerry, it was not because each Democratic voter made an independent judgment on Kerry's behalf. It was in large part because of a widespread perception that other people were flocking to Kerry. Duncan Watts's amusing account (2004) is worth quoting at length: A few weeks before the Iowa caucuses, Kerry's campaign seemed dead, but then he unexpectedly won Iowa, then New Hampshire, and then primary after primary. How did this happen?... When everyoneis looking to someone else for an opinion—trying, for example, to pick the Democratic candidate they think everyone else will pick—it's possible that whatever information other people might have gets lost, and instead we get a cascade of imitation that, like a stampeding herd, can start for no apparent reason and subsequently go in any direction with equal likelihood.... We think of ourselves as autonomous individuals, each driven by our internal abilities and desires and therefore solely responsible for our own behavior, particularly when it comes to voting. No voter ever admits—even to herself—that she chose Kerry because he won New Hampshire. Social Nudges as Choice Architecture The general lesson is clear. If choice architects want to shift behavior and to do so with a nudge, they might simply inform people about what other people are doing. Sometimes the practices of others are surprising, and hence people are much affected by learning what they are. Consider four examples.

4

WHEN DO WE NEED A NUDGE?

We have seen that people perform amazing feats but also commit ditzy blunders. What's the best response? Choice architecture and its effects cannot be avoided, and so the short answer is an obvious one, call it the golden rule of libertarian paternalism: offer nudges that are most likely to help and least likely to inflict harm.* A slightly longer answer is that people will need nudges for decisions that are difficult and rare, for which they do not get prompt feedback, and when they have trouble translating aspects of the situation into terms that they can easily understand. In this chapter we try to put some flesh on these points. We begin by specifying the kinds of situations in which people are least likely to make good choices. We then turn to questions about the potential magic of markets and ask whether and when free markets and open competition will tend to exacerbate rather than mitigate the effects of human frailty. The key point here is that for all their virtues, markets often give companies a strong incentive to cater to (and profit from) human frailties, rather than to try to eradicate them or to minimize their effects. We have seen that people perform amazing feats but also commit ditzy blunders. What's the best response? Choice architecture and its effects cannot be avoided, and so the short answer is an obvious one, call it the golden rule of libertarian paternalism: offer nudges that are most likely to help and least likely to inflict harm.* A slightly longer answer is that people will need nudges for decisions that are difficult and rare, for which they do not get prompt feedback, and when they have trouble translating aspects of the situation into terms that they can easily understand. In this chapter we try to put some flesh on these points. We begin by specifying the kinds of situations in which people are least likely to make good choices. We then turn to questions about the potential magic of markets and ask whether and when free markets and open competition will tend to exacerbate rather than mitigate the effects of human frailty. The key point here is that for all their virtues, markets often give companies a strong incentive to cater to (and profit from) human frailties, rather than to try to eradicate them or to minimize their effects.

Fraught Choices Suppose you are told that a group of people will have to make some choice in the near future. You are the choice architect. You are trying to decide how to design the choice environment, what kinds of nudges to offer, and how subtle the nudges should be. What do you need to know to design the best possible choice environment? Benefits Now—Costs Later We have seen that predictable problems arise when people must make decisions that test their capacity for self-control. Many choices in life, such as whether to wear a blue shirt or a white one, lack important selfcontrol elements. Self-control issues are most likely to arise when choices and their consequences are separated in time. At one extreme are what might be called investment goods, such as exercise, flossing, and dieting. For these goods the costs are borne immediately, but the benefits are delayed. For investment goods, most people err on the side of doing too little. Although there are some exercise nuts and flossing freaks, it seems safe to say that not many people are resolving on New Year's Eve to floss less next year and to stop using the exercise bike so much. At the other extreme are what might be called sinful goods: smoking, alcohol, and jumbo chocolate doughnuts are in this category. We get the pleasure now and suffer the consequences later. Again we can use the New Year's resolution test: how many people vow to smoke more cigarettes, drink more martinis, or have more chocolate donuts in the morning next year? Both investment goods and sinful goods are prime candidates for nudges. Most (nonanorexic) people do not need any special encouragement to eat another brownie, but they could use some help exercising more. Degree of Difficulty Nearly everyone over the age of six can tie shoelaces, play a respectable game of tic-tac-toe, and spell the word cat. But only a few of us can tie a decent bow tie, play a masterly game of chess, or spell (much less pronounce) the name of the psychologist Mihály Csíkszentmihályi. Of course, we learn to cope with the harder problems. We can buy a pretiedFraught Choices Suppose you are told that a group of people will have to make some choice in the near future. You are the choice architect. You are trying to decide how to design the choice environment, what kinds of nudges to offer, and how subtle the nudges should be. What do you need to know to design the best possible choice environment? Benefits Now—Costs Later We have seen that predictable problems arise when people must make decisions that test their capacity for self-control. Many choices in life, such as whether to wear a blue shirt or a white one, lack important selfcontrol elements. Self-control issues are most likely to arise when choices and their consequences are separated in time. At one extreme are what might be called investment goods, such as exercise, flossing, and dieting. For these goods the costs are borne immediately, but the benefits are delayed. For investment goods, most people err on the side of doing too little. Although there are some exercise nuts and flossing freaks, it seems safe to say that not many people are resolving on New Year's Eve to floss less next year and to stop using the exercise bike so much. At the other extreme are what might be called sinful goods: smoking, alcohol, and jumbo chocolate doughnuts are in this category. We get the pleasure now and suffer the consequences later. Again we can use the New Year's resolution test: how many people vow to smoke more cigarettes, drink more martinis, or have more chocolate donuts in the morning next year? Both investment goods and sinful goods are prime candidates for nudges. Most (nonanorexic) people do not need any special encouragement to eat another brownie, but they could use some help exercising more. Degree of Difficulty Nearly everyone over the age of six can tie shoelaces, play a respectable game of tic-tac-toe, and spell the word cat. But only a few of us can tie a decent bow tie, play a masterly game of chess, or spell (much less pronounce) the name of the psychologist Mihály Csíkszentmihályi. Of course, we learn to cope with the harder problems. We can buy a pretied

bow tie, read a book about chess, and look up the spelling of Csíkszentmihályi on the Web (then copy and paste every time we have to use the name). We use spell checkers and spreadsheets to help with harder problems. But many problems in life are quite difficult, and often there is no technology as easy as a spell checker available to help. We are more likely to need more help picking the right mortgage than choosing the right loaf of bread.

Frequency Even hard problems become easier with practice. Both of us have managed to learn how to serve a tennis ball into the service court with reasonable regularity (and in Sunstein's case, even velocity), but it took some time. The first time people try to execute this motion, they are lucky if the ball goes over the net, much less into the service box. Practice makes perfect (or at least better). Unfortunately, some of life's most important decisions do not come with many opportunities to practice. Most students choose a college only once. Outside of Hollywood, most of us choose a spouse, well, not more than two or three times. Few of us get to try many different careers. And outside of science fiction, we get one chance to save for retirement (though we can make some adjustments along the way). Generally, the higher the stakes, the less often we are able to practice. Most of us buy houses and cars not more than once or twice a decade, but we are really practiced at grocery shopping. Most families have mastered the art of milk inventory control, not by solving the relevant mathematical equation but through trial and error.

None of this is to say that the government should be telling people whom to marry or what to study. This is a book about libertarian paternalism. At this stage we just want to stress that rare, difficult choices are good candidates for nudges. Feedback Even practice does not make perfect if people lack good opportunities for learning. Learning is most likely if people get immediate, clear feedback after each try. Suppose you are practicing your putting skills on the practice green. If you hit ten balls toward the same hole, it is easy to get a sense of how hard you have to hit the ball. Even the least talented golfers will soon learn to gauge distance under these circumstances. Suppose instead you were putting the golf balls but not getting to see where they were going. In that environment, you could putt all day and never get any better. Alas, many of life's choices are like practicing putting without being able to see where the balls end up, and for one simple reason: the situation is not structured to provide good feedback. For example, we usually get feedback only on the options we select, not the ones we reject. Unless people go out of their way to experiment, they may never learn about alternatives to the familiar ones. If you take the long route home every night, you may never learn there is a shorter one. Long-term processes rarely provide good feedback. Someone can eat a high-fat diet for years without having any warning signs until the heart attack. When feedback does not work, we may benefit from a nudge.None of this is to say that the government should be telling people whom to marry or what to study. This is a book about libertarian paternalism. At this stage we just want to stress that rare, difficult choices are good candidates for nudges. Feedback Even practice does not make perfect if people lack good opportunities for learning. Learning is most likely if people get immediate, clear feedback after each try. Suppose you are practicing your putting skills on the practice green. If you hit ten balls toward the same hole, it is easy to get a sense of how hard you have to hit the ball. Even the least talented golfers will soon learn to gauge distance under these circumstances. Suppose instead you were putting the golf balls but not getting to see where they were going. In that environment, you could putt all day and never get any better. Alas, many of life's choices are like practicing putting without being able to see where the balls end up, and for one simple reason: the situation is not structured to provide good feedback. For example, we usually get feedback only on the options we select, not the ones we reject. Unless people go out of their way to experiment, they may never learn about alternatives to the familiar ones. If you take the long route home every night, you may never learn there is a shorter one. Long-term processes rarely provide good feedback. Someone can eat a high-fat diet for years without having any warning signs until the heart attack. When feedback does not work, we may benefit from a nudge.Knowing What You Like Most of us have a good sense of whether we prefer coffee ice cream to vanilla, Frank Sinatra to Bob Dylan, and mysteries to science fiction. These are examples for which we have had the time to sample the alternatives and learn about our tastes. But suppose that you have to forecast your preferences for the unfamiliar, such as when dining for the first

time in a country with an exotic cuisine. Smart tourists often rely on others (waiters, for example) for help: "Most foreigners like x and hate y." Even in less exotic locales, it can be smart to let someone else choose for you. Two of the best restaurants in Chicago (Alinea and Charlie Trotter's) give their diners the fewest choices. At Alinea diners just decide whether they want fifteen very small plates or twenty-five tiny ones. At Charlie Trotter's, the diner is asked only whether to limit the dining to vegetables or not. (In both, one is asked about dietary restrictions and allergies.) The benefit of having so little choice is that the chef is authorized to cook you things you would never have thought to order.time in a country with an exotic cuisine. Smart tourists often rely on others (waiters, for example) for help: "Most foreigners like x and hate y." Even in less exotic locales, it can be smart to let someone else choose for you. Two of the best restaurants in Chicago (Alinea and Charlie Trotter's) give their diners the fewest choices. At Alinea diners just decide whether they want fifteen very small plates or twenty-five tiny ones. At Charlie Trotter's, the diner is asked only whether to limit the dining to vegetables or not. (In both, one is asked about dietary restrictions and allergies.) The benefit of having so little choice is that the chef is authorized to cook you things you would never have thought to order.

It is particularly hard for people to make good decisions when they have trouble translating the choices they face into the experiences they will have. A simple example is ordering a dish from a menu in a language you do not understand. But even when you do know the meaning of the words being used, you may not be able to translate the alternatives you are considering into terms that make the slightest sense to you. Take the problem of choosing a mutual fund for your retirement portfolio. Most investors (including us) would have trouble knowing how to compare a "capital appreciation" fund with a "dynamic dividend" fund, and even if the use of those words were made comprehensible, the problem would not be solved. What an investor needs to know is how a choice between those funds affects her spending power during retirement under various scenarios—something even an expert armed with a good software package and complete knowledge of the portfolios held by each fund can have trouble analyzing. The same problem arises for the choice among health plans; we may have little understanding of the effects of our selection. If your daughter gets a rare disease, will she be able to see a good specialist? How long will she have to wait in line? When people have a hard time predicting how their choices will end up affecting their lives, they have less to gain by numerous options and perhaps even by choosing for themselves. A nudge might be welcomed. Markets: A Mixed Verdict The discussion thus far suggests that people may most need a good nudge for choices that have delayed effects; those that are difficult,infrequent, and offer poor feedback; and those for which the relation between choice and experience is ambiguous. A natural question is whether free markets can solve people's problems, even under such circumstances. Often market competition will do a lot of good. But in some cases, companies have a strong incentive to cater to people's frailties and to exploit them. Notice first that many insurance products have all of the fraught features that we have sketched. The benefits from holding the insurance are delayed, the probability of having a claim is hard to analyze, consumers do not get useful feedback on whether they are getting a good return on their insurance purchases, and the mapping from what they are buying to what they are getting can be ambiguous. But the insurance market is competitive, so a natural question to ask is whether market forces can be relied upon to "solve" the problem of fraught choices. Let's imagine two different worlds. In one world, Econworld, all the consumers are Econs and they have no problem with difficult choices. All quantitative decisions, including insurance purchases, are a piece of cake for them. (Econs are part actuary.) The other world is called Humanworld, and in this world some of the consumers are Humans, who have all the features that generally characterize the tribe, while the rest are Econs. In both worlds, there are well-functioning markets and at least some perfectly rational firms that have hired Econs as managers. The key question is whether the insurance purchases in Humanworld will be the same as the ones in Econworld. In other words, do well-functioning markets render the humanness of the Humans irrelevant? To analyze this question, let's start with a simple example inspired by a wonderful poem by Shel Silverstein (1974) entitled "Smart." The poem is fun as well as brilliant, so if you have a computer nearby, we suggest that you type "Smart" and "Shel Silverstein" into Google and read the poem now.* We will wait for you to get back before continuing.

For those of you reading this on a plane (or too lazy to get up out of bed), the poem's tale is simple. The child narrator explains that his father gave him a dollar bill, which he wisely traded for two quarters because he (unlike his dumb trading partners) knows that two is more than one. He continues trading—the two quarters for three dimes; three dimes for four nickels; and finally four nickels for five pennies. Finally the son comes back to his father to report on his series of brilliant trades. When he does so, he reports that his father was "too proud of [him] to speak." Suppose that some Humans in a well-functioning market economy prefer two quarters to one dollar because two is more than one. What happens to these quarter lovers? Are they harmed? And do they influence market prices? The answers to these questions depend a bit on how dumb the quarter lovers are, but let's suppose that while they prefer two quarters to one dollar, they still prefer more quarters to fewer quarters (since they love quarters). That means that while they would, in principle, be willing to trade two quarters for a dollar, they won't have to do that, because banks (among others) will compete for their business, and will be happy to give them four quarters for each dollar. Of course the quarter lovers will think they are getting a great deal on this trade, but as long as there is competition in the provision of quarters, quarters will still sell for twenty-five cents and the irrational love of quarters will be essentially harmless to those who have this affliction. The example is obviously an extreme one, but many markets are not so different from this situation. Most of the time, competition ensures that price serves as a good signal of quality. Usually (but not always) the fiftydollar bottles of wine are better than the twenty-dollar bottles. And irrational consumers will not alter the market as long as they do not predominate. So if some people choose wine by how much they like the label, they will not be harmed, but if many people start to do that, then wine with attractive labels will be overpriced. For irrational consumers to be protected there has to be competition. Sometimes that competition does not exist. Consider the case of extended warranties on small appliances, typically a bad deal for consumers. To take a specific hypothetical example, suppose that a cell phone costs two hundred dollars. The cell phone has a free warranty for the first year, but the cell phone company offers, for twenty dollars, an extended warranty for

the second year of the phone's life. After that the consumer plans to buy a new phone. Suppose that the chance that the phone will break during the second year is 1 percent, so on average consumers will get two dollars' worth of benefits from having this policy—but the price of the extended warranty is twenty dollars in order to include a normal profit to the insurer and a kickback (er, commission) to the salesperson at the cell phone store. Of course, Econs understand all this and thus do not purchase extended warranties. But Humans want extended warranties, perhaps because the salesman offers the "friendly" advice that the extended warranty is a good idea, or perhaps because they mistakenly think that cell phones break 15 percent of the time rather than 1 percent, or perhaps because they just think that it's "better to be safe than sorry." What happens? Do market forces drive these unduly expensive extended warranties from the market? Or does competition drive the price of the extended warranties down to two dollars, the expected value of the claims? The answers to these questions are no and no. (Before we explain, notice that extended warranties are plentiful in the real world and that many people buy them. Hint: Don't.)* On our assumptions, the extended warranty is a product that simply should not exist. If Humans realized that they were paying twenty dollars for two dollars' worth of insurance, they would not buy the insurance. But if they do not realize this, markets cannot and will not unravel the situation. Competition will not drive the price down, in part because it takes the salesperson a while to persuade someone to pay twenty dollars for two dollars' worth of insurance, and in part because it is difficult for third parties to enter this market efficiently. You might think that firms could educate people not to buy the warranty, and indeed they might. But why should firms do that? If you are buying something that you shouldn't, how do I make any money persuading you not to buy it? There is a general point here. If consumers have a less than fully rational belief, firms often have more incentive to cater to that belief than to eradicate it. When many people were still afraid of flying, it was common to see airline flight insurance sold at airports at exorbitant prices. There were no booths in airports selling people advice not to buy such insurance. In many markets, firms will be competing for the same consumers but will be offering products that are not merely different but that directly oppose each other. Some firms sell cigarettes; others sell products that help you quit smoking. Some firms sell fast food; others sell diet advice. If all consumers are Econs, then there is no reason to worry about which of these competing interests wins. But if some of the consumers are Humans who sometimes make bad choices (as judged by themselves, of course), then all of us may have an interest in which set of firms wins the battle. Government can, of course, outlaw some kinds of activities, but as libertarian paternalists we prefer to nudge—and we are keenly aware that governments are populated by Humans. What can be done to help? In the next chapter we describe our primary tool: choice architecture.

5

CHOICE ARCHITECTURE

Early in Thaler's career, he was teaching a class on managerial decision making to business school students. Students would sometimes leave class early to go for job interviews (or a golf game) and would try to sneak out of the room as surreptitiously as possible. Unfortunately for them, the only way out of the room was through a large double door in the front, in full view of the entire class (though not directly in Thaler's line of sight). The doors were equipped with large, handsome wood handles, vertically mounted cylindrical pulls about two feet in length. When the students came to these doors, they were faced with two competing instincts. One instinct says that to leave a room you push the door. The other instinct says, when faced with large wooden handles that are obviously designed to be grabbed, you pull. It turns out that the latter instinct trumps the former, and every student leaving the room began by pulling on the handle. Alas, the door opened outward. At one point in the semester, Thaler pointed this out to the class, as one embarrassed student was pulling on the door handle while trying to escape the classroom. Thereafter, as a student got up to leave, the rest of the class would eagerly wait to see whether the student would push or pull. Amazingly, most still pulled! Their Automatic Systems triumphed; the signal emitted by that big wooden handle simply could not be screened out. (And when Thaler would leave that room on other occasions, he sheepishly found himself pulling too.) Those doors are bad architecture because they violate a simple psychological principle with a fancy name: stimulus response compatibility. The idea is that you want the signal you receive (the stimulus) to be consistent with the desired action. When there are inconsistencies, performance suffers and people blunder. Consider, for example, the effect of a large, red, octagonal sign that said GO. The difficulties induced by such incompatibilities are easy to show experimentally. One of the most famous such demonstrations is the Stroop (1935) test. In the modern version of this experiment people see words flashed on a computer screen and they have a very simple task. They press the right button if they see a word that is displayed in red, and press the left button if they see a word diplayed in green. People find the task easy and can learn to do it very quickly with great accuracy. That is, until they are thrown a curve ball, in the form of the word green displayed in red, or the word red displayed in green. For these incompatible signals, response time slows and error rates increase. A key reason is that the Automatic System reads the word faster than the color naming system can decide the color of the text. See the word green in red text and the nonthinking Automatic System rushes to press the left button, which is, of course, the wrong one. You can try this for yourself. Just get a bunch of colored crayons and write a list of color names, making sure that most of the names are not the same as the color they are written in. (Better yet, get a nearby kid to do this for you.) Then name the color names as fast as you can (that is, read the words and ignore the color): easy, isn't it? Now say the color that the words are written in as fast as you can and ignore the word itself: hard, isn't it? In tasks like this, Automatic Systems always win over Reflective ones. Although we have never seen a green stop sign, doors such as the ones described above are commonplace, and they violate the same principle. Flat plates say "push me" and big handles say "pull me," so don't expect people to push big handles! This is a failure of architecture to accommodate basic principles of human psychology. Life is full of products that suffer from such defects. Isn't it obvious that the largest buttons on a television remote control should be the power, channel, and volume controls? Yet how many remotes do we see that have the volume control the same size as the "input" control button (which if pressed accidentally can cause the picture to disappear)? It is possible, however, to incorporate human factors into design, as Don Norman's wonderful book The Design of Everyday Things (1990) illustrates. One of his best examples is the design of a basic four-burner stove (Figure 5.1). Most such stoves have the burners in a symmetric arrangement, as in the stove pictured at the top, with the controls arranged in a linear fashion below. In this set-up, it is easy to get confused about which knob controls the front burner and which controls the back, and many pots and pans have been burned as a result. The other two designs we have illustrated are only two of many better possibilities. Norman's basic lesson is that designers need to keep in mind that the users of their objects are Humans who are confronted every day with myriad choices and cues. The goal of this chapter is to develop the same idea for choice architects. If you indirectly influence the choices other people make, you are a choice architect. And since the choices you are influencing are going to be made by Humans, you will want your architecture to reflect a good understanding of how humans behave. In particular, you will want to ensure that the Automatic System doesn't get all confused. In this chapter, we offer some basic principles of good (and bad) choice architecture. Defaults: Padding the Path of Least Resistance For reasons we have discussed, many people will take whatever option requires the least effort, or the path of least resistance. Recall the discussion of inertia, status quo bias, and the "yeah, whatever" heuristic. All these forces imply that if, for a given choice, there is a default option—an option that will obtain if the chooser does nothing—then we can expect a large number of people to end up with that option, whether or not it is good for them. And as we have also stressed, these behavioral tendencies toward doing nothing will be reinforced if the default option comes with some implicit or explicit suggestion that it represents the normal or even the recommended course of action. Defaults are ubiquitous and powerful. They are also unavoidable in the sense that for any node of a choice architecture system, there must be an associated rule that determines what happens to the decision maker if she does nothing. Of course, usually the answer is that if I do nothing, nothing changes; whatever is happening continues to happen. But not always.

Some dangerous machines, such as chain saws and lawn mowers, are designed with "dead man switches," so that once you are no longer gripping the machine, it stops. When you leave your computer alone for a while to answer a phone call, nothing is likely to happen until you have talked for a long time, at which point the screen saver comes on, and if you neglect the computer long enough, it may lock itself. Of course, you can choose how long it takes before your screen saver comes on, but implementing that choice takes some action. Your computer probably came with a default time lag and a default screen saver. Chances are, those are the settings you still have. Many organizations in both the public and the private sector have discovered the immense power of default options. Successful businesses certainly have. Remember the idea of automatic renewal for magazine subscriptions? If renewal is automatic, many people will subscribe, for a long time, to magazines they don't read. Business offices at most magazines are aware of that fact. When you download a new piece of software, you will often have numerous choices to make. Do you want the "regular" or "custom" installation? Normally, one of the boxes is already checked, indicating it is the default. Which boxes do the software suppliers check? Two different motives are readily apparent: helpful and self-serving. In the helpful category would be making the regular installation the default if most users will have trouble with the custom installation. In the self-serving category would be making the default a willingness to receive emails with information about new products. In our experience, most software comes with helpful defaults regarding the type of installation, but many come with self-serving defaults on other choices. We will have more to say about motives later. For now, note that not all defaults are selected to make the chooser's life easier or better. The choice of the default can be quite controversial. Here is one example. An obscure portion of the No Child Left Behind Act requires that school districts supply the names, addresses, and telephone numbers of students to the recruiting offices of branches of the armed forces. However, the law stipulates that "a secondary school student or the parent of the student may request that the student's name, address, and telephone listing not be released without prior written parental consent, and the local educational agency or private school shall notify parents of the option to make a request and shall comply with any request." Some school districts, such as Fairport, New York, interpreted this law as allowing them to implement an "opt-in" policy. That is, parents were notified that they could elect to make their children's contact information available, but if they did not do anything, this information would be withheld. This reading of the law did not meet with the approval of then–Secretary of Defense Donald Rumsfeld. The Defense and Education Departments sent a letter to school districts asserting that the law required an optout implementation. Only if parents actively requested that the contact information on their children be withheld would that option apply. In typical bureaucratic language, the departments contended that the relevant laws "do not permit LEA's [local educational agencies] to institute a policy of not providing the required information unless a parent has affirmatively agreed to provide the information."1 Both the Defense Department and the school districts realized that opt-in and opt-out policies would lead to very different outcomes. Not surprisingly, much hue and cry ensued. We discuss a similarly touchy subject involving defaults in our chapter on organ donations. We have emphasized that default rules are inevitable—that private institutions and the legal system cannot avoid choosing them. In some cases, though not all, there is an important qualification to this claim. The choice architect can force the choosers to make their own choice. We call this approach "required choice" or "mandated choice." In the software example, required choice would be implemented by leaving all the boxes unchecked, and by requiring that at every opportunity one of the boxes be checked in order for people to proceed. In the case of the provision of contact information to the military recruiters, one could imagine a system in which all students (or their parents) are required to fill out a form indicating whether they want to make their contact information available. For emotionally charged issues like this one, such a policy has considerable appeal, because people might not want to be defaulted into an option that they might hate (but fail to reject because of inertia, or real or apparent social pressure). We believe that required choice, favored by many who like freedom, is sometimes the best way to go. But consider two points about that approach. First, Humans will often consider required choice to be a nuisance or worse, and would much prefer to have a good default. In the software example, it is really helpful to know what the recommended settings are. Most users do not want to have to read an incomprehensible manual in order to determine which arcane setting to elect. When choice is complicated and difficult, people might greatly appreciate a sensible default. It is hardly clear that they should be forced to choose. Second, required choosing is generally more appropriate for simple yesor-no decisions than for more complex choices. At a restaurant, the default option is to take the dish as the chef usually prepares it, with the option to ask that certain ingredients be added or removed. In the extreme, required choosing would imply that the diner has to give the chef the recipe for every dish she orders! When choices are highly complex, required choosing may not be a good idea; it might not even be feasible.

Expect Error Humans make mistakes. A well-designed system expects its users to err and is as forgiving as possible. Some examples from the world of real design illustrate this point: · In the Paris subway system, Le Métro, users insert a paper card the size of a movie ticket into a machine that reads the card, leaves a record on the card that renders it "used," and then spits it out from the top of the machine. The cards have a magnetic strip on one side but are otherwise symmetric. On Thaler's first visit to Paris, he was not sure how to use the system, so he tried putting the card in with the magnetic strip face up and was pleased to discover that it worked. He was careful thereafter to insert the card with the strip face up. Many years and trips to Paris later, he was proudly demonstrating to a visiting friend the correct way to use the Metro system when his wife started laughing. It turns out that it doesn't matter which way you put the card into the machine! In stark contrast to Le Métro is the system used in most Chicago parking garages. When entering the garage, you put your credit card into a machine that reads it and remembers you. Then when leaving, you must insert the card again into another machine at the exit. This involves reaching out of the car window and inserting the card into a slot. Because credit cards are not symmetric, there are four possible ways to put the card into the slot (face up or down, strip on the right or left). Exactly one of those ways is the right way. And in spite of a diagram above the slot, it is very easy to put the card in the wrong way, and when the card is spit back out, it is not immediately obvious what caused the card to be rejected or to recall which way it was inserted the first time. Both of us have been stuck for several painful minutes behind some idiot who was having trouble with this machine, and have to admit to having occasionally been the idiot that is making all the people behind him start honking. · Over the years, automobiles have become much friendlier to their Human operators. If you do not buckle your seat belt, you are buzzed. If you are about to run out of gas, a warning sign appears and you might be beeped. If you need an oil change, your car might tell you. Many cars come with an automatic switch for the headlights that turns them on when you are operating the car and off when you are not, eliminating the possibility of leaving your lights on overnight and draining the battery. But some error-forgiving innovations are surprisingly slow to be adopted. Take the case of the gas tank cap. On any sensible car the gas cap is attached by a piece of plastic, so that when you remove the cap you cannot possibly drive off without it. Our guess is that this bit of plastic cannot cost more than ten cents. Once some firm had the good idea to include this feature, what excuse can there ever have been for building a car without one? Leaving the gas cap behind is a special kind of predictable error psychologists call a "postcompletion" error.2 The idea is that when you have finished your main task, you tend to forget things relating to previous steps. Other examples include leaving your atm card in the machine after getting your cash, or leaving the original in the copying machine after getting your copies. Most atms (but not all) no longer allow this error because you get your card back immediately. Another strategy, suggested by Norman, is to use what he calls a "forcing function," meaning that in order to get what you want, you have to do something else first. So if in order to get your cash, you have to remove the card, you will not forget to do so. · Another automobile-related bit of good design involves the nozzles for different varieties of gasoline. The nozzles that deliver diesel fuel are too large to fit into the opening on cars that use gasoline, so it is not possible to make the mistake of putting diesel fuel in your gasoline-powered car (though it is still possible to make the opposite mistake). The same principle has been used to reduce the number of errors involving anesthesia. One study found that human error (rather than equipment failure) caused 82 percent of the "critical incidents." A common error was that the hose for one drug was hooked up to the wrong delivery port, so the patient received the wrong drug. This problem was solved by designing the equipment so that the gas nozzles and connectors were different for each drug. It became physically impossible to make this previously frequent mistake.3 · A major problem in health care is called "drug compliance." Many patients, especially the elderly, are on medicines they must take regularly, and in the correct dosage. So here is a choice-architecture question. If you are designing a drug, and you have complete flexibility, how often would you want your patients to have to take their medicine? If we rule out a one-time dose administered immediately by the doctor (which would be best on all dimensions but is often technically infeasible), then the next-best solution is a medicine taken once a day, preferably in the morning. It is clear why once a day is better than twice (or more) a day, because the more often you have to take the drug, the more opportunities you have to forget. But frequency is not the only concern; regularity is also important. Once a day is much better than once every other day, because the Automatic System can be educated to think: "My pill(s) every morning, when I wake up." Taking the pill becomes a habit, and habits are controlled by the Automatic System. By contrast, remembering to take your medicine every other day is beyond most of us. (Similarly, meetings that occur every week are easier to remember than those that occur every other week.) Some medicines are taken once a week, and most patients take this medicine on Sundays (because that day is different from other days for most people and thus easy to associate with taking one's medicine). Birth control pills present a special problem along these lines, because they are taken every day for three weeks and then skipped for one week. To solve this problem and to make the process automatic, the pills are typically sold in a special container that contains twenty-eight pills, each in a numbered compartment. Patients are instructed to take a pill every day, in order. The pills for days twenty-two through twenty-eight are placebos whose only role is to facilitate compliance for Human users.

Give Feedback The best way to help Humans improve their performance is to provide feedback. Well-designed systems tell people when they are doing well and when they are making mistakes. Some examples: · Digital cameras generally provide better feedback to their users than film cameras. After each shot, the photographer can see a (small) version of the image just captured. This eliminates all kinds of errors that were common in the film era, from failing to load the film properly (or at all), to forgetting to remove the lens cap, to cutting off the head of the central figure of the picture. However, early digital cameras failed on one crucial feedback dimension. When a picture was taken, there was no audible cue to indicate that the image had been captured. Modern models now include a very satisfying but completely fake "shutter click" sound when a picture has been taken. (Some cell phones, aimed at the elderly, include a fake dial tone, for similar reasons.) · An important type of feedback is a warning that things are going wrong, or, even more helpful, are about to go wrong. Our laptops warn us to plug in or shut down when the battery is dangerously low. But warning systems have to avoid the problem of offering so many warnings that they are ignored. If our computer constantly nags us about whether we are sure we want to open that attachment, we begin to click "yes" without thinking about it. These warnings are thus rendered useless. · The Department of Homeland Security's color-coded terror alert system is a nice illustration of feedback that would be useless even if it weren't incessant. When walking through an American airport any time since 2002, one is bound to hear the following announcement: "The Department of Homeland Security has raised the National Threat Advisory to Orange." Aside from putting our toiletries into a one-quart zip-lock bag, exactly what actions are we expected to take as a result of this warning? A look at the Homeland Security Web site provides the answer. We are told: "All Americans should continue to be vigilant, take notice of their surroundings, and report suspicious items or activities to local authorities immediately." Weren't we supposed to be doing this at level Yellow? It is a safe bet that these announcements are useless. (Much more useful would be a supply of one-quart zip-lock bags for absentminded travelers; and many airports do in fact provide these.) · Feedback can be improved in many activities. Consider the simple task of painting a ceiling. This task is more difficult than it might seem because ceilings are nearly always painted white, and it can be hard to see exactly where you have painted. Later, when the paint dries, the patches of old paint will be annoyingly visible. How to solve this problem? Some helpful person invented a type of ceiling paint that goes on pink when wet but turns white when dry. Unless the painter is so colorblind that he can't tell the difference between pink and white, this solves the problem. Understanding "Mappings": From Choice to Welfare Some tasks are easy, like choosing a flavor of ice cream; other tasks are hard, like choosing a medical treatment. Consider, for example, an ice cream shop where the varieties differ only in flavor, not calories or other nutritional content. Selecting which ice cream to eat is merely a matter of choosing the one that tastes best. If the flavors are all familiar, such as vanilla, chocolate, and strawberry, most people will be able to predict with considerable accuracy the relation between their choice and their ultimate consumption experience. Call this relation between choice and welfare a mapping. Even if there are some exotic flavors, the ice cream store can solve the mapping problem by offering a free taste. Choosing among treatments for some disease is quite another matter. Suppose you are told that you have been diagnosed with prostate cancer and must choose among three options: surgery, radiation, and "watchful waiting" (which means do nothing for now). Each of these options comes with a complex set of possible outcomes regarding side effects of treatment, quality of life, length of life, and so forth. Comparing the options involves making such trade-offs as the following: Would I be willing to risk a one-third chance of impotence or incontinence in order to increase my life expectancy by 3.2 years? This is a hard decision at two levels. First, the patient is unlikely to know these trade-offs, and second, he is unlikely to be able to imagine what life would be like if he were incontinent. Yet here are two scary facts about this scenario. First, most patients decide which course of action to take in the very meeting at which their doctor breaks the bad news about the diagnosis. Second, the treatment option they choose depends strongly on the type of doctor they see.4 (Some specialize in surgery, others in radiation. None specialize in watchful waiting. Guess which option we suspect might be underutilized?) The comparison between ice cream and treatment options illustrates the concept of mapping. A good system of choice architecture helps people to improve their ability to map and hence to select options that will make them better off. One way to do this is to make the information about various options more comprehensible, by transforming numerical information into units that translate more readily into actual use. If I am buying apples to make into apple cider, it helps to know the rule of thumb that it takes three apples to make one glass of cider. Take the example of choosing a digital camera. Cameras advertise their megapixels, and the impression created is certainly that the more megapixels the better. This assumption is itself subject to question, because photos taken with more megapixels take up more room on the camera's storage device and a computer's hard drive. But what is really problematic for consumers is translating megapixels (not the most intuitive concept) into what they care about. Is it worth paying an additional hundred dollars to go from four to five megapixels? Suppose instead that manufacturers listed the largest print size recommended for a given camera. Instead of being given the options of three, five, or seven megapixels, consumers might be told that the camera can produce quality photos at 4 × 6 inches, 9 × 12, or "poster size." Often people have a problem in mapping products into money. For simple choices, of course, such mappings are trivial. If a Snickers bar costs one dollar, you can easily figure out how much it costs to have a Snickers bar every day. But do you know how much it costs you to use your credit card? Among the fees you may be paying are: (a) an annual fee for the privilege of using the card (common for cards that provide benefits such as frequent flyer miles); (b) an interest rate for borrowing money (that depends on your deemed credit worthiness); (c) a fee for making a payment late (and you may end up making more late payments than you anticipate); (d) interest on purchases made during the month that is normally not charged if your balance is paid off but begins if you make your payment one day late; and (e) a charge for buying things in currencies other than dollars. Credit cards are not alone in having complex pricing schemes that are neither transparent nor comprehensible to consumers. Think about mortgages, cell phone calling plans, and auto insurance policies, just to name a few. For these and related domains, we propose a very mild form of government regulation, a species of libertarian paternalism that we call recap: Record, Evaluate, and Compare Alternative Prices. Here is how recap would work in the cell phone market. The government would not regulate how much issuers could charge for services, but it would regulate their disclosure practices. The central goal would be to inform customers of every kind of fee that currently exists. This would not be done by printing a long unintelligible document in fine print. Instead, issuers would be required to make public their fee schedule in a spreadsheetlike format that would include all relevant formulas. Suppose you are in Toronto and your cell phone rings. How much is it going to cost you to answer it? What if you download some email? All these prices would be embedded in the formulas. This is the price disclosure part of the regulation. The usage disclosure requirement would be that once a year, issuers would have to send their customers a complete listing of all the ways they had used the phone and all the fees that had been incurred. This report would be sent two ways, by mail and, more important, electronically. The electronic version would also be stored and downloadable on a secure Web site. Producing the recap reports would cost cell phone carriers very little, but the reports would be extremely useful for customers who want to compare the pricing plans of cell phone providers, especially after they had received their first annual statement. Private Web sites similar to existing travel sites would emerge to allow an easy way to compare services. With just a few quick clicks, a shopper would easily be able to import her usage data from the past year and find out how much various carriers would have charged, given her usage patterns.* Consumers who are new to the product (getting a cell phone for the first time, for example) would have to guess usage information for various categories, but the following year they could take full advantage of the system's capabilities. We will see that in many domains, from mortgages and credit cards to energy use to Medicare, a recap program could greatly improve people's ability to make good choices. Structure Complex Choices People adopt different strategies for making choices depending on the size and complexity of the available options. When we face a small number of well-understood alternatives, we tend to examine all the attributes of all the alternatives and then make trade-offs when necessary. But when the choice set gets large, we must use alternative strategies, and these can get us into trouble. Consider, for example, Jane, who has just been offered a job at a company located in large city far from where she is living now. Compare two choices she faces: which office to select and which apartment to rent. Suppose Jane is offered a choice of three available offices in her workplace. A reasonable strategy for her to follow would be to look at all three offices, note the ways they differ, and then make some decisions about the importance of such attributes as size, view, neighbors, and distance to the nearest rest room. This is described in the choice literature as a "compensatory" strategy, since a high value for one attribute (big office) can compensate for a low value for another (loud neighbor). Obviously, the same strategy cannot be used to pick an apartment. In a large city like Los Angeles, thousands of apartments are available. If Jane ever wants to start working, she will not be able to visit each apartment and evaluate them all.

Instead, she is likely to simplify the task in some way. One strategy to use is what Amos Tversky (1972) called "elimination by aspects." Someone using this strategy first decides what aspect is most important (say, commuting distance), establishes a cutoff level (say, no more than a thirty-minute commute), then eliminates all the alternatives that do not come up to this standard. The process is repeated, attribute by attribute (no more than $1,500 per month; at least two bedrooms; dogs permitted), until either a choice is made or the set is narrowed down enough to switch over to a compensatory evaluation of the "finalists." When people are using a simplifying strategy of this kind, alternatives that do not meet the minimum cutoff scores may be eliminated even if they are fabulous on all other dimensions. So, for example, an apartment that is a thirty-five-minute commute will not be considered even if it has a dynamite view and costs two hundred dollars a month less than any of the alternatives. Social science research reveals that as the choices become more numerous and/or vary on more dimensions, people are more likely to adopt simplifying strategies. The implications for choice architecture are related. As alternatives become more numerous and more complex, choice architects have more to think about and more work to do, and are much more likely to influence choices (for better or for worse). For an ice cream shop with three flavors, any menu listing those flavors in any order will do just fine, and effects on choices (such as order effects) are likely to be minor because people know what they like. As choices become more numerous, though, good choice architecture will provide structure, and structure will affect outcomes. Consider the example of a paint store. Even ignoring the possibility of special orders, paint companies sell more than two thousand colors that you can apply to the walls in your home. It is possible to think of many ways of structuring how those paint colors are offered to the customer. Imagine, for example, that the paint colors were listed alphabetically. Artic White might be followed by Azure Blue, and so forth. While alphabetical order is a satisfactory way to organize a dictionary (at least if you have a guess as to how a word is spelled), it is a lousy way to organize a paint store. Instead, paint stores have long used something like a paint wheel, with color samples ordered by similarity: all the blues are together, next to the greens, and the reds are located near the oranges, and so forth. The problem of selection is made considerably easier by the fact that people can see the actual colors, especially since the names of the paints are spectacularly uninformative. (On the Benjamin Moore Paints Web site, three similar shades of beige are called "Roasted Sesame Seed," "Oklahoma Wheat," and "Kansas Grain.") Thanks to modern computer technology and the World Wide Web, many problems of consumer choice have been made simpler. The Benjamin Moore Paints Web site not only allows the consumer to browse through dozens of shades of beige, but it also permits the consumer to see (within the limitations of the computer monitor) how a particular shade will work on the walls with the ceiling painted in a complementary color. And the variety of paint colors is small compared to the number of books sold by Amazon (millions) or Web pages covered by Google (billions). Many companies such as Netflix, the mail-order dvd rental company, succeed in part because of immensely helpful choice architecture. Customers looking for a movie to rent can easily search movies by actor, director, genre, and more, and if they rate the movies they have watched, they can also get recommendations based on the preferences of other movie lovers with similar tastes, a method called "collaborative filtering." You use the judgments of other people who share your tastes to filter through the vast number of books or movies available in order to increase the likelihood of picking one you like. Collaborative filtering is an effort to solve a problem of choice architecture. If you know what people like you tend to like, you might well be comfortable in selecting products you don't know, because people like you tend to like them. For many of us, collaborative filtering is making difficult choices easier.

A cautionary note: surprise and serendipity can be fun for people, and good for them too, and it may not be entirely wonderful if our primary source of information is about what people like us like. Sometimes it's good to learn what people unlike us like—and to see whether we might even like that. If you like the mystery writer Robert B. Parker (and we agree that he's great), collaborative filtering will probably direct you to other mystery writers (we suggest trying Lee Child, by the way), but why not try a little Joyce Carol Oates, or maybe even Henry James? If you're a Democrat, and you like books that fit your predilections, you might want to see what Republicans think; no party can possibly have a monopoly on wisdom. Public-spirited choice architects—those who run the daily newspaper, for example—know that it's good to nudge people in directions that they might not have specifically chosen in advance. Structuring choice sometimes means helping people to learn, so they can later make better choices on their own.5 Incentives Our last topic is the one with which most economists would have started: prices and incentives. Though we have been stressing factors that are often neglected by traditional economic theory, we do not intend to suggest that standard economic forces are unimportant. This is as good a point as any to state for the record that we believe in supply and demand. If the price of a product goes up, suppliers will usually produce more of it and consumers will usually want less of it. So choice architects must think about incentives when they design a system. Sensible architects will put the right incentives on the right people. One way to start to think about incentives is to ask four questions about a particular choice architecture: Who uses? Who chooses? Who pays? Who profits? Free markets often solve all of the key problems by giving people an incentive to make good products and to sell them at the right price. If the market for sneakers is working well, there will be a lot of competition; bad sneakers will be driven from the market and the good ones will be priced in accordance with people's tastes. Sneaker producers and sneaker purchasers have the right incentives. But sometimes incentive conflicts arise. Consider a simple case. When we go for our weekly lunch, each of us chooses his own meal and pays for what he eats. The restaurant serves us our food and keeps our money. No conflicts here. Now suppose we decide to take turns paying for lunch. Sunstein now has an incentive to order something more expensive on the weeks that Thaler is paying, and vice versa. (In this case, though, friendship introduces a complication; one of us may well order something cheaper if he knows that the other is paying. Sentimental but true.) Many markets (and choice architecture systems) are replete with incentive conflicts. Perhaps the most notorious is the U.S. health care system. The patient receives the health care services that are chosen by his physician and paid for by the insurance company, with everyone from equipment manufacturers to drug companies to malpractice lawyers taking a piece of the action. Those with different pieces have different incentives, and the results may not be ideal for either patients or doctors. Of course, this point is obvious to anyone who thinks about these problems. But as usual, it is possible to elaborate and enrich the standard analysis by remembering that the agents in the economy are Humans. To be sure, even mindless Humans demand less when they notice that the price has gone up. But will they notice? Only if they are really paying attention. The most important modification that must be made to a standard analysis of incentives is salience. Do the choosers actually notice the incentives they face? In free markets, the answer is usually yes, but in important cases the answer is no. Consider the example of members of an urban family deciding whether to buy a car. Suppose their choices are to take taxis and public transportation or to spend ten thousand dollars to buy a used car, which they can park on the street in front of their home. The only salient costs of owning this car will be the weekly stops at the gas station, occasional repair bills, and a yearly insurance bill. The opportunity cost of the ten thousand dollars is likely to be neglected. (In other words, once they purchase the car, they tend to forget about the ten thousand dollars and stop treating it as money that could have been spent on something else.) In contrast, every time the family uses a taxi the cost will be in their face, with the meter clicking every few blocks. So a behavioral analysis of the incentives of car ownership will predict that people will underweight the opportunity costs of car ownership, and possibly other less salient aspects such as depreciation, and may overweight the very salient costs of using a taxi.* An analysis of choice architecture systems must make similar adjustments. Of course, salience can be manipulated, and good choice architects can take steps to direct people's attention to incentives. The telephones at the insead School of Business in France are programmed to display the running costs of long-distance phone calls. If we want to protect the environment and to increase energy independence, similar strategies could be used to make costs more salient. Suppose the thermostat in your home was programmed to tell you the cost per hour of lowering the temperature a few degrees during the heat wave. This would probably have more effect on your behavior than quietly raising the price of electricity, a change that will be experienced only at the end of the month when the bill comes. Suppose in this light that government wants to increase energy conservation. Increases in the price of electricity will surely have an effect; making the increases salient will have a greater effect. Cost-disclosing thermostats might have a greater impact than (modest) price increases designed to decrease use of electricity. In some domains, people may want the salience of gains and losses treated asymmetrically. For example, no one would want to go to a health club that charged its users on a "per step" basis on the Stairmaster. However, many Stairmaster users enjoy watching the "calories burned" meter while they work out (especially since those meters seem to give generous estimates of calories actually burned). Even better, for some, might be a pictorial display that indicated the calories one had burned in terms of food: after ten minutes one had earned only a bag of carrots but after forty minutes a large cookie. We have sketched six principles of good choice architecture. As a concession to the bounded memory of our readers, we thought it might be useful to offer a mnemonic device to help recall the six principles. By rearranging the order, and using one small fudge, the following emerges. iNcentives Understand mappings Defaults Give feedback Expect error Structure complex choices Voilà: NUDGES With an eye on these nudges, choice architects can improve the outcomes for their Human users.

6

SAVE MORE TOMORROW

In 2005 the personal savings rate for Americans was negative for the first time since 1932 and 1933—the Great Depression years. On average, American households spent more than they earned and borrowed more than they saved. Increased borrowing rates were fueled by substantial growth in home equity loans and in credit card debt. For many Americans, savings rates, especially retirement savings, are woefully low, if not zero. Consider, for example, the case of Tony Snow, the former White House press secretary, who resigned at age fifty-two in 2007 to return to the private sector. He said his motivation for leaving was financial. "I ran out of money," he told reporters. "We took out a loan when I came to the White House, and that loan is now gone. So I'm going to have to pay the bills." Before serving as press secretary, Snow worked a much more lucrative gig as a Fox News Channel anchor. But he arrived at the White House not having learned Retirement 101 lessons. "Snow conceded: 'As a matter of fact, I was even too dopey to get in on a 401(k).'"1 The fact that many people are not saving for retirement exacerbates the looming problems facing the Social Security system. As all politicians know but few are willing to say, we will eventually have to bite the bullet in order to make Social Security solvent, through some combination of tax increases or benefit cuts. Americans would be better able to deal with this problem if they were saving more on their own. And indeed, the government has often passed laws designed to encourage personal savings, typically by creating tax-favored savings accounts such as iras and 401(k)s.

Such programs are well intended, but many Americans who are eligible for such plans do not take full advantage of them. What can be done to help? We will be offering two central suggestions. The first is automatic enrollment in savings plans; the second is the Save More Tomorrow program. To understand why these nudges would work, and why they are not part of the usual economics repertoire, we need to step back a bit. The standard economic theory of saving for retirement is both elegant and simple. People are assumed to calculate how much they are going to earn over the rest of their lifetime, figure out how much they will need when they retire, and then save up just enough to enjoy a comfortable retirement without sacrificing too much while they are still working. As a guideline for how to think sensibly about saving, this theory is excellent, but as an approach to how people actually behave, the theory runs into two serious problems. First, it assumes that people are capable of solving a complicated mathematical problem in order to figure out how much to save. Without good computer software, even a trained economist would find this problem daunting. The truth is that we know few economists (and no lawyers) who have made a serious attempt at doing it (even with software).* The second problem with the theory is that it assumes that people have enough willpower to implement the relevant plan. Under the standard theory, flashy sports cars or nice vacations never distract people from their project of saving up for a condo in Florida. In short, the standard theory is about Econs, not Humans. For most of their time on earth, Humans did not have to worry much about saving for retirement, because most people did not live long enough to have much of a retirement period. In most societies, those who did make it to old age were cared for by their children. In the twentieth century, the combination of rising life expectancies and geographical dispersion of families made it necessary for people to think about providing for their own retirement income rather than depending on their children to do it. Both employers and governments began to take steps to help with this problem, with Bismarck's early social security program in Germany leading the way in 1889.2 Early pension plans tended to be defined-benefit plans. In such plans, participants are entitled to a benefit that depends on a specific formula, typically based on the participant's salary and the number of years the participant was a member of the plan. In a typical private plan, a worker is entitled to receive a benefit that is a proportion of the salary paid over the last few years of work, the proportion depending on years of service. Most public social security systems, including that of the United

States, are also defined-benefit plans. Your Social Security check depends on the amount you have paid in taxes and the number of years you have worked. The payouts are even adjusted for inflation, so you know exactly what you will be paid (unless Congress changes its mind, as it is entitled to do; the Constitution does not protect your right to Social Security benefits). From the perspective of choice architecture, defined-benefit plans have one large virtue: they are forgiving to even the most mindless of Humans. With Social Security, the only decision a worker has to make is when to start receiving benefits. The only form to fill out is the one where you write down your Social Security number, and you have to fill it out if you want to get paid! In the private sector, defined-benefit plans are also easy and forgiving, as long as the worker keeps working for the same employer, and the employer stays in business. The decision about when to retire is not so easy, but it is only one decision; the same is true for the decision about when to start claiming Social Security benefits. We discuss that decision, and how the government might offer some useful nudges, at the end of this chapter. While a defined-benefit world can be an easy one for someone who stays in one job her entire life, employees who change jobs frequently can end up with virtually no retirement benefits, because there is often a minimum employment period (such as five years) before any benefits are vested (that is, owned by the employee). Defined-benefit plans are also expensive for employers to administer. Many old firms are switching over to definedcontribution plans, and nearly all new firms offer only defined-contribution plans. Under a defined-contribution plan, employees, and sometimes employers, make specific contributions to a tax-sheltered account in the

employee's name. The benefits received by employees in retirement depend on the decisions they make about how much to save and how to invest. Defined-contribution plans, such as 401(k) plans in the United States, have many desirable features for modern workers. The plans are completely portable, so a worker is free to move from one job to another. The plans are also flexible, giving employees the opportunity to adjust their savings and investment decisions to reflect their own financial situation and tastes. However, defined-contribution plans are not very forgiving. Employees have to get around to joining, to figuring out how much to save, to managing their portfolio over a period of years, and then to deciding what to do with the proceeds when they finally retire. People can find the whole process frightening, and many seem to be making a mess of the task. Are People

Saving Enough? Of course, a key question is whether people are saving enough. Are they? This turns out to be a complex and controversial question. For one thing, economists do not agree about how much saving is appropriate, because they do not agree on the right level of post-retirement income. Some economists argue that people should aim to have retirement income that is at least as high as the income enjoyed when working, because retirement years offer the opportunity for such time-intensive expensive activities as travel. Retired people also have to worry about growing health care costs. Others claim that retirees can use their greater time to live a more economical lifestyle: saving the money once spent on business clothes, taking the time to shop carefully and prepare meals at home, and taking advantage of senior discounts. We do not take a strong position on this debate, but consider a few points. It seems clear that the costs of saving too little are greater than the costs of saving too much. There are many ways to cope with having saved too much—from retiring earlier than expected, to taking up golf, to traveling to Europe, to spoiling the grandchildren. Coping in the opposite direction is less pleasant. Second, we can say for sure that some people in our society are definitely saving too little—namely, those employees who are not participating at all in their retirement plan, or are saving a low percentage of their income after having reached their forties (or older). These folks could clearly use a nudge. For what it is worth, many employees say that they "should" be saving more. In one study, 68 percent of 401(k) participants said that their savings rate is "too low," 31 percent said that their savings rate is "about right," and only 1 percent said their savings rate is "too high." Economists tend to belittle such statements, and partly for good reason. It is easy to say that you "should" be doing many good things—dieting, exercising, spending more time with your children—and people's actions may tell us more than their words. After all, few of the participants who say they should be saving more make any changes in their behavior. But such statements are not meaningless or random. Many people announce an intention to eat less and exercise more next year, but few say they hope to smoke more next year or watch more sitcom reruns. We interpret the statement "I should be saving (or dieting, or exercising) more" to imply that people would be open to strategies that would help them achieve these goals. In other words, they are open to a nudge. They might even be grateful for one. Enrollment Decisions: Nudging People to Join The first step in participating in a defined contribution plan, such as a 401(k), is to enroll. Most workers should find joining the plan very attractive.

Contributions are tax deductible, accumulations are tax deferred, and in many plans the employer matches at least part of the contributions of the employee. For example, a common plan feature is that the employer will match 50 percent of the employee's contributions up to some threshold, such as 6 percent of salary. This match is virtually free money. Taking full advantage of the match should be a no-brainer for all but the most impatient or cash-strapped households. Nevertheless, enrollment rates in such plans are far from 100 percent. Roughly 30 percent of employees eligible to join a 401(k) plan fail to enroll.3 Typically, younger, less-educated, and lower-income employees are less likely to join, but even high-paid workers sometimes fail to sign up, as the Tony Snow example illustrates. To be sure, there are situations, say for young workers with other pressing financial needs, in which it could be sensible not to join even with an employer match. But in many cases, the failure to join is simply a blunder. One extreme example comes from the United Kingdom, where some defined-benefit plans do not require any employee contributions and are fully paid for by the employer. They do require employees to take action to join the plan. Data on twenty-five such plans reveal that scarcely half of the eligible employees (51 percent) signed up!4 This is equivalent to not bothering to cash your paycheck. Some older American workers are also turning down "free money." To have this free money option, a worker must meet three qualifications: he needs to be more than 591/2 years old, so that he faces no tax penalty when he withdraws funds from his retirement account; his firm has to offer a matching contribution (meaning that the firm contributes something if the employee does); and his employer has to allow employees to withdraw funds from their retirement accounts while still working. For such employees, joining the plan is a sure profit opportunity because they can join, then immediately withdraw their contributions without any penalty, yet keep the employer match. Nonetheless, a study finds that up to 40 percent of eligible workers either do not join the plan at all or do not save enough to get the full match.5 These extreme examples are just the clearest cases in which people's failure to join a plan is foolish beyond a doubt. In many other cases, workers take months or years to join the plan, and it is a reasonable assumption that most of these workers are just spacing out or procrastinating rather than making a reasoned decision that they have a better use for their money. How can we nudge these people to join more quickly?* Making Savings Automatic An obvious answer is to change the default rule. As things now stand, the default is nonenrollment; you have to do a little work to get into a retirement plan. When workers are first eligible to join (sometimes immediately upon employment), they usually receive a form to fill out. Employees who want to join must decide how much to put aside, and how to allocate their investments among the funds offered in the plan. Forms can be a headache, and many employees just put them aside. An alternative is to adopt automatic enrollment. Here's how it works. When an employee first becomes eligible, she receives a form indicating that she will be enrolled in the plan (at a specified savings rate and asset allocation), unless she actively fills out a form asking to opt out. Automatic enrollment has proven to be an extremely effective way to increase enrollment in U.S. defined-contribution plans.6 In one plan studied in an early paper by Brigitte Madrian and Dennis Shea (2001), participation rates under the opt-in approach were barely 20 percent after three months of employment, gradually increasing to 65 percent after thirty-six months. But when automatic enrollment was adopted, enrollment of new employees jumped to 90 percent immediately and increased to more than 98 percent within thirty-six months. Automatic enrollment thus has two effects: participants join sooner, and more participants join eventually. Does automatic enrollment merely overcome workers' inertia, helping them make the choice they would actually prefer? Or does automatic enrollment somehow seduce workers into saving when they would prefer to be spending? One telling bit of evidence is that under automatic enrollment, very few employees drop out of the plan once enrolled. In a study of four companies that adopted automatic enrollment, the fraction of 401(k) participants who dropped out of the plan in the first year was only 0.3 to 0.6 percentage points higher than it had been before automatic enrollment was introduced.7 Although the low dropout rate is, of course, partly due to inertia, the fact that so few people drop out does suggest that workers are not suddenly discovering, to their dismay, that they are saving more than they had wanted. Forced Choosing and More Simplicity An alternative to automatic enrollment is simply to require every employee to make an active decision about whether to join the plan. If a worker is eligible when he is first hired, he might be required to check a "yes" or a "no" box for participation in order to get paid. With required choosing in place, employees have to state their preferences, and there is no default option. As compared with the usual opt-in approach (you are not enrolled unless you decide to fill out the forms), required choosing should increase participation rates. One company switched from an opt-in regime to active decisions and found that participation rates increased by about 25 percentage points.8 A related strategy is to simplify the enrollment process. One study tested this idea by analyzing a simplified enrollment form.9 New employees were handed enrollment cards during orientation with a "yes" box for joining the plan at a 2 percent savings rate and a preselected asset allocation. Employees did not have to spend time choosing a savings rate and asset allocation; they could just check the "yes" box for participation. As a result, participation rates during the first four months of employment jumped from 9 percent to 34 percent. These simplified enrollment procedures are very much in the spirit of the "channel factors" we mentioned in Chapter 3. People really do want to join the plan, and if you dig a channel for them to slide down that removes the seemingly tiny barriers that are getting in their way, the results can be quite dramatic. While automatic enrollment or "quick" enrollment makes the process of joining a retirement plan less daunting, expanding the number of funds available to participants can have the opposite effect. One study finds that the more options in the plan, the lower the participation rates.10 This finding should not be surprising. With more options, the process becomes more confusing and difficult, and some people will refuse to choose at all. Choosing Contribution Rates Both automatic enrollment programs and forced choosing plans typically adopt a relatively low default savings rate of 2 or 3 percent, and a very conservative investment choice, such as a money market account. It turns out that many employees continue saving at the default rate of 2 percent. This rate is usually far too low to provide enough money for retirement. Many employees also remain in the default investment fund, and they lose a lot of money as a result. We will turn to investment strategies in One indication that people need help in picking a savings rate and don't realize that they need the help is that most people spend very little time on this important financial decision. One survey found that 58 percent spent less than one hour determining both their contribution rate and investment decisions.11 Most people spend more time than that picking a new tennis racket or television set. Apparently, many people are using some simple shortcuts. In many plans, participants are asked to state a desired savings rate as a percentage of pay. Many people simply pick a "round number," typically 5, 10, or 15 percent of income. Of course, there is no sensible reason why the correct percentage of your income to save would be an exact multiple of 5. Another common rule of thumb is to contribute to a retirement account the minimum amount necessary to get the full employer match. If the employer matches employees' contributions up to 6 percent of pay, then many employees contribute 6 percent. If participants are behaving this way, then firms wanting to encourage employee savings might alter their matching formula to help workers. Changing the match formula from 50 percent on the first 6 percent of pay to 30 percent on the first 10 percent of pay would probably increase contribution rates. Those who use the match threshold as a rule of thumb would save more with a higher matching threshold. And by picking a round number as the threshold, the company would nudge those who use the "multiple of 5" heuristic. Education What else can employers do, if they want more employees to enroll in retirement plans, contribute an amount that will build a reasonable retirement nest egg, and allocate the funds among assets in an appropriately diversified way? Education is the obvious answer, and many employers have tried to educate their employees to make better decisions. Unfortunately, the evidence does not suggest that education is, in and of itself, an adequate solution. One large employer, having offered its employees the chance to switch from a defined-benefit to a defined-contribution plan, provided a free financial education program.12 The employer measured the effectiveness of this education by administering a before-and-after test of financial literacy. The quiz used a true/false format, so random answers would receive, on average, a score of 50 percent. Before the education, the average score of the employees was 54; after the education, the average score crept up to 55. Teaching is hard! Employees often leave educational seminars excited about saving more but then fail to follow through on their plans. One study found that at the seminar everyone expressed an interest in saving more, but only 14 percent actually joined the savings plan. This was an improvement, but not a large one, over the 7 percent of comparable employees who did not attend a seminar and joined the savings plan.13 Studies of the effects of attendance at a "benefit fair" also find only a small effect on participation in a taxdeferred savings account.14 Save More Tomorrow Although automatic enrollment is effective at getting new and young workers to enroll sooner than they would have otherwise, participants tend to stick with the default contribution rate, which is typically quite low. To mitigate this problem, consider a program of automatic escalation of contributions, developed by Thaler and his frequent collaborator Shlomo Benartzi, called Save More Tomorrow. Save More Tomorrow is a choice-architecture system that was constructed with close reference to five psychological principles that underlie human behavior: · Many participants say that they think they should be saving more, and plan to save more, but never follow through. · Self-control restrictions are easier to adopt if they take place some time in the future. (Many of us are planning to start diets soon, but not today.) · Loss aversion: people hate to see their paychecks go down. · Money illusion: losses are felt in nominal dollars (that is, not adjusted for inflation, so a dollar in 1995 is seen as worth the same as a dollar in 2005). · Inertia plays a powerful role.

7
NAÏVE INVESTING

We have been exploring the first part of saving for retirement: joining a plan and deciding how much to invest. We now turn to the allimportant second part: how to invest the money. Once again the switch from defined-benefit to defined-contribution plans has given employees more control, more options, and more responsibility. Although solving the problem of how much to save is hard, choosing the right portfolio is even harder. In fact, in an effort to make what we say about it comprehensible, we will simplify the actual problems people face. Just take our word for it that things are really even harder than we are letting on. The first question investors face is this: how much risk to take? As a rule, riskier investments such as stocks (also called equities) earn higher rates of return than safer investments such as government bonds or money market accounts. Choosing the appropriate mix of stocks and bonds (and possibly other assets such as real estate) is called the asset-allocation decision. If an investor is willing to allocate more of her money to risky assets, then she will usually make more money, but of course more risk means taking the chance that returns will actually be lower. And the decision of how much to save is related in complex ways to the willingness to bear risk. Someone who insists on investing everything in a safe money market account that earns a modest rate of interest had better be saving quite a bit if she wants to have enough to have a comfortable retirement. Suppose an investor chooses to invest 70 percent of her money in stocks

and 30 percent in bonds. That choice still leaves open many specific questions of how the money is to be invested. In retirement accounts, most investors do not choose stocks individually but rather invest via mutual funds. The funds themselves differ in how risky they are, and how much they charge for their services. Some funds are specialized (investing only in companies in a particular industry or country, for example) while others invest broadly. There are also funds designed for one-stop shopping, blending a mix of stocks and bonds together. Should investors form their own blend or choose a fund blended for them? Further complicating the mix is that some companies offer employees the opportunity to invest in the company's own shares. Should workers want to own shares in the company they work for? Making all these decisions is hard work (or should be if done carefully), and participants might be excused for thinking that having made these choices they can relax and look forward to a wonderful retirement. However, all these decisions should be revisited periodically. An investor who chose to invest half her money in stocks and half in bonds could find that stocks have shot up and two-thirds of her portfolio is now invested in stocks. Should something be done? Should some of the stocks be sold to get back to the 50–50 allocation? Or should she put more of her money in stocks, because they seem to be doing so well? Econs have no trouble with all these decisions, but Humans can easily become flummoxed. As we will see, Human investors are making all kinds of mistakes in this domain, and could benefit from a more helpful and forgiving investment choice architecture. Stocks and Bonds How should you decide how much of your portfolio should be invested in stocks? (Do you know how much of your portfolio is invested in stocks?) Of course you know that stocks have historically earned higher rates of return, but by how much? Consider the eighty-year period from 1925 to 2005. If you had invested a dollar in U.S. Treasury bills (short-term, completely safe, bonds issued by the government), you would have turned your dollar into $18, a 3.7 percent rate of return per year. That does not seem bad until you realize

that just to keep up with inflation you had to earn 3.0 percent per year. If you had invested your money in longer-term bonds, your dollar would have become $71, a 5.5 percent rate of return, which is quite a bit better. But if you had invested in mutual funds that held shares in the largest American companies (such as an S&P 500 index fund), your dollar would have grown into $2,658, a 10.4 percent rate of return, and if you had invested in a broad portfolio of the stocks of smaller companies, you could have earned even more. In economics jargon, in which stocks are referred to as equities, the difference in the returns between Treasury bills and equities is called the "equity premium." This premium is considered to be compensation for the greater risk associated with investing in stocks. Whereas Treasury bills are guaranteed by the federal government, and are essentially risk free, investments in stocks are risky. Although the average rate of return has been 10 percent, there have been years when stocks have fallen by more than 30 percent, and on October 19, 1987, stock indexes fell 20 percent or more all around the world in a single day. How would Econs decide how much of their portfolio to invest in stocks? An Econ would make a trade-off between risk and return that would be based on his preferences about retirement income. That is, he would decide whether the possibility of being, say, 25 percent richer is worth the risk of being 15 percent poorer. Needless to say, even if it occurred to Humans to think about the problem this way, they would not know how to make the necessary calculations. The decisions they do make will differ from those of Econs in two ways. First, they will be unduly influenced by short-term fluctuations, and second, their decisions are likely to be based on rules of thumb. Let's consider each in turn. Countin' Your Money While Sittin' at the Table Recall from Chapter 1 that Humans are loss averse. Roughly speaking, they hate losses about twice as much as they like gains. With this in mind, consider the behavior of two investors, Vince and Rip. Vince is a stock broker, and he has constant access to information about the value of all of his investments. By habit, at the end of each day, he runs a little program to calculate how much money he has made or lost that day. Being Human, when Vince loses five thousand dollars in a day he is miserable— about as miserable as he is happy at the end of a day when he gains ten thousand dollars. How does Vince feel about investing in stocks? Very nervous! On a daily basis, stocks go down almost as often as they go up, so if you are feeling the pain of losses much more acutely than the pleasure of gains, you will hate investing in stocks. Now compare Vince with his friend and client Rip, a scion of the old Van Winkle family. In a visit to his doctor Rip is told that he is about to follow the long-standing family tradition and will soon go to sleep for twenty years. The doctor tells him to make sure he has a comfortable bed, and suggests that Rip call his broker to make sure his asset allocation is where it should be. How will Rip feel about investing in stocks? Quite calm! Over a twenty-year period, stocks are almost certain to go up. (There is no twenty-year period in history in which stocks have declined in real value, or have been outperformed by bonds.) So Rip calls Vince, tells him to put all his money in stocks, and sleeps like a baby. The lesson from the story of Vince and Rip is that attitudes toward risk depend on the frequency with which investors monitor their portfolios. As Kenny Rogers advises in his famous song "The Gambler": "You never count your money when you're sittin' at the table, / There'll be time enough for countin' when the dealin's done." Many investors do not heed this good advice and invest too little of their money in stocks. We believe this qualifies as a mistake, because if the investors are shown the evidence on the risks of stocks and bonds over a long period of time, such as twenty years (the relevant horizon for many investors), they choose to invest nearly all of their money in stocks.1 Market Timing: Buy High, Sell Low Throughout the 1990s, people were increasing the proportion of their retirement money invested in stocks, both in terms of the percentage of money contributed each year and the account balances held. What produced this shift in behavior? One (rather remote) possibility was that investors had spent the decade poring over finance and economics journals, had learned that stock returns had been substantially higher than bond returns over the past century or so, and so decided to invest more in stocks.

The other (considerably more likely) possibility is that investors had come to believe that stocks only go up—or that even if stock prices fall, that is just another buying opportunity because they quickly rise again. The stock market provided an opportunity to test these competing hypotheses during the 2000–2002 market turndown. One way to analyze the market-timing ability of investors is to see how their asset-allocation decisions (that is, the proportion of their portfolios invested in stocks) changed over time. The problem with this approach is that, as we have already mentioned, most people hardly ever change their portfolios unless they change jobs and have to fill out a new set of forms. So a better way to judge what people are thinking is to look at the percentage of money being invested in stocks by new participants who have just made the decision. We have data on one large group of such participants who were customers of plans administered by the Vanguard mutual fund company. In 1992 new participants were allocating 58 percent of their assets to equities, and by 2000 that percentage had risen to 74. In the next two years, however, the allocation to equities for new participants fell back to 54 percent. Their market timing was backward. They were heavily buying stocks when stock prices were high, and then selling stocks when their prices were low. We observe similar behavior in the asset allocations within equities. Some plans allow investors to choose funds that specialize in particular industries or sectors. We have data from one such plan that offered its employees the option of investing in a technology fund. In 1998, in the early phase of the rapid run-up in the shares of technology companies, only 12 percent of employees invested in the technology fund. By 2000, when technology share prices were peaking, 37 percent of employees had money invested in that fund. After the fall in these share prices, the number of new participants investing in the technology fund had dropped back down to 18 percent by 2001. Again, participants were buying into the technology fund most aggressively at the peak, and selling after prices had fallen. Rules of Thumb Even the most sophisticated investors can sometimes find the decision about how to invest their money daunting, and they resort to 122 MONEY simple rules of thumb. Take the example of the financial economist and Nobel laureate Harry Markowitz, one of the founders of modern portfolio theory. When asked about how he allocated his retirement account, he confessed: "I should have computed the historic covariances of the asset classes and drawn an efficient frontier. Instead . . . I split my contributions fifty-fifty between bonds and equities."2 Markowitz was not alone. In the mid-1980s most educators had a defined-contribution pension plan provided by a company that goes by its initials, tiaa-cref. At that time the plan had only two options—tiaa, which invests in fixed-income securities such as bonds, and cref, which invests mostly in stocks. More than half of the participants in this plan, many of them professors of some sort, selected exactly a 50–50 split between these two options. One of these 50–50 investors was Sunstein. Notwithstanding his long-standing friendship with Thaler, who many years ago told him that over the long haul cref was a better bet than tiaa, he hasn't changed a thing. It is on his list of things to do, right after canceling those magazine subscriptions. Of course, an even split between stocks and bonds is not a self-evidently dumb portfolio, but if the initial allocation is never changed (or "rebalanced," in the finance parlance), then over time the mix of assets will depend on the rates of return. For example, Sunstein has been investing equal amounts into tiaa and cref for more than twenty-five years, and he now has well over 60 percent of his money in cref. The reason is that stocks have significantly outperformed bonds over the time period he has been a professor. If he had invested most of his money in stocks, he would have done a lot better. Markowitz's strategy can be viewed as one example of what might be called the diversification heuristic. "When in doubt, diversify." Don't put all your eggs in one basket. In general, diversification is a great idea, but there is a big difference between sensible diversification and the naïve kind. A special case of this rule of thumb is what might be called the "1/n" heuristic: "When faced with 'n' options, divide assets evenly across the options."3 Put the same number of eggs in each basket. Naïve diversification apparently starts young. Consider the following clever experiment conducted by Daniel Read and George Loewenstein on Halloween night.4 The "subjects" were trick-or-treaters. In one condiNAÏVE INVESTING 123 tion, the children approached two adjacent houses and were offered a choice between the same two candy bars (Three Musketeers and Milky Way) at each house. In the other condition, they approached a single house, where they were asked to "choose whichever two candy bars you like." Large piles of both candies were displayed to ensure that the children would not think it was rude to take two of the same. The two conditions produced quite different results. In the house with both kinds of candy, every child selected one of each candy. In contrast, only 48 percent of the children picked one of each candy when they were choosing in sequence in two houses. Although the consequences of picking two different candies are minimal (Three Musketeers and Milky Way are both pretty good), naïve diversification in portfolio selection can have more significant consequences on what people do, and on how much money they end up having. In a revealing study, university employees were asked how they would invest their retirement money if they had just two funds to choose from.5 In one condition, one of the funds invested entirely in stocks, the other in bonds. Most of the participants chose to invest their money half and half, achieving an asset allocation of 50 percent stocks. Another group was told that one fund invested entirely in stocks and the other "balanced" fund invested half in stocks and half in bonds. People in this group could have also have invested 50 percent of their money in stocks by putting all their money in the balanced fund. Instead, they followed the 1/n rule and divided their money evenly between the two funds—ending up with mostly stocks. People in a third group were given a choice between a balanced fund and a bond fund. Well, you can guess what they did. This result implies that the set of funds offered in a particular plan can greatly influence the choices participants make. To test this prediction, Benartzi and Thaler (2001) examined behavior in retirement saving plans of 170 companies. They found that the more stock funds the plan offered, the greater was the percentage of participants' money invested in stocks. Many plans have attempted to help participants deal with the difficult problem of portfolio construction by offering "lifestyle" funds that blend stocks and bonds in a way designed to meet the needs of different levels of risk tolerance. For example, an employer might offer three lifestyle funds: conservative, moderate, and aggressive. These funds are already diversi124 MONEY fied, so individuals need pick only the fund that fits their risk preference. Some funds also adjust the asset allocation with the age of the participant. Such a fund assortment is a good idea and represents an excellent set of default options (if the fees are reasonable). But when the funds are just included in a mix of other funds, many people appear not to understand how to use them. For example, few participants put all of their money into one of these funds, even though that is the mission for which they were designed. This is the equivalent of a not-particularly-hungry diner going to a restaurant that offers a set five-course menu and ordering the set menu plus the roast duck and a dessert. One study investigated the behavior of participants in a plan that offered three lifestyle funds and six other funds (an index fund, a growth fund, a bond fund, and so on).6 Curiously, the participants who invested in the conservative lifestyle fund allocated just 31 percent to that fund, dividing the rest among the other funds. Because the menu of other funds is dominated by stock funds, the resulting stock exposure for those investing in the conservative fund was 77 percent. These participants end up with a fairly aggressive portfolio, probably without being aware of it. Company Stock Consider the case of Charlie Prestwood, who spent his best years in the Texas energy business. He started at the bottom in 1967, sweeping sidewalks and emptying trash cans for a company called Houston Natural Gas. He was still there in 1985 when the company's ceo, a Houston native named Kenneth Lay, engineered its sale to a Nebraska-based competitor called Internorth. Lay helped restructure the new company, Enron, which distributed electricity and gas throughout the United States. "My job on the pipeline was keeping the gas flowing to our customers," says Prestwood. "I worked all my life devoted to it." Life as an Enron employee was good. Prestwood's annual salary rose steadily to sixty-five thousand dollars, with additional retirement benefits paid in Enron stock. When Houston Natural and Internorth had merged, all of Prestwood's investments were automatically converted to Enron stock. He continued to set aside money in the company's retirement fund, buying even more stock. Internally, the company relentlessly promoted NAÏVE INVESTING 125 employee stock ownership. Newsletters touted Enron's growth as "simply stunning," and Lay, at company events, urged employees to buy more stock. To Prestwood, it didn't seem like a problem that his future was tied directly to Enron's. Enron had committed to him, and he was showing his gratitude. "To me, this is the American way, loyalty to your employer," he says.

Prestwood was loyal to the bitter end. When he retired in 2000, he had accumulated 13,500 shares of Enron stock, worth $1.3 million at their peak. Then, at age sixty-eight, Prestwood suddenly lost his entire Enron nest egg. He now survives on a previous employer's pension of $521 a month and a Social Security check of $1,294. "There ain't no such thing as a dream anymore," he says. He lives on a three-acre farm north of Houston willed to him as a baby in 1938 after his mother died. "I hadn't planned much for the retirement. Wanted to go fishing, hunting. I was gonna travel a little." Now he'll sell his family's land. Has to, he says. He is still paying off his mortgage.7 In some respects, Prestwood's case is not unusual. Often people do not diversify at all, and sometimes employees invest a lot of their money in their employer's stock. Amazing but true: five million Americans have more than 60 percent of their retirement savings in company stock.8 This concentration is risky on two counts. First, a single security is much riskier than the portfolios offered by mutual funds. Second, as employees of Enron and WorldCom discovered the hard way, workers risk losing both their jobs and the bulk of their retirement savings all at once. Remarkably, many employees still do not think these risks apply to their own employer. There are three problems here. First, employees do not seem to understand the risk-and-return profile of company stock. When the Boston Research Group surveyed 401(k) participants in 2002, it found that despite a high level of awareness of the Enron experience, half of the respondents thought that their own company stock carried the same or less risk than a money market fund. Another recent survey found that only a third of the respondents who owned company stock realized that it is riskier than a "diversified fund with many different stocks."9 Second, plan participants tend to extrapolate past performance into the future. Employees of companies whose stock has been performing well over the previous ten years tend to invest much more in company stock 126 MONEY than employees at firms that were performing poorly. But this past performance is no prediction of the future. You might think that employees have especially good information about their firm's future prospects, but a careful study by Shlomo Benartzi (2001) finds otherwise. Specifically, there is no correlation between the allocation to company stock and subsequent stock performance. So workers at firms such as Enron, whose stock had been flying high, kept pouring more of their money into the company's stock (with encouragement from management) right up until the day the company imploded, and the stock became worthless. Third, employees who receive an employer's matching contribution in company stock view that contribution as implicit advice. In particular, those who are required to take the employer's match in the form of company stock allocate 29 percent of their discretionary contributions—that is, the money they have control over—to company stock. By contrast, those who have the option, but not the requirement, to take the employer's match in the form of company stock allocate only 18 percent of their own funds to company stock.10 How risky is it to hold the shares of a single stock rather than a diversified portfolio? According to estimates by the economist Lisa Meulbroek (2002), a dollar in company stock is worth less than half the value of a dollar in a mutual fund! In other words, when firms foist company stock onto their employees, it is like paying them fifty cents on the dollar. The upshot is that, in general, workers would be much better off with a diversified mutual fund than with company stock. (Hint: if you have more than 10 percent of your retirement money invested in the company you work for, diversify as quickly as possible.) What nudges can help with this problem?11 We prefer libertarian approaches, but we must acknowledge that a nonlibertarian argument can be made for limiting the percentage of an employee's retirement portfolio that is held in company stock—say, to 10 percent. Bills to this effect have been introduced in Congress. A more libertarian alternative is to treat company stock like any other investment in a 401(k) plan. Company stock in defined-contribution plans now enjoys an important benefit under the principal federal fiduciary law, an extremely important and largely unintelligible statute named the Employee Retirement Income Security Act of 1974 (erisa). Erisa sets forth three fiduciary principles for retirementNAÏVE INVESTING 127 plan investments: the exclusive benefit rule, requiring that plans be managed exclusively for the benefit of participants; the prudence rule, requiring that plan assets be invested according to a "prudent investor" standard; and the diversification rule, requiring that plan assets be diversified so as to minimize the risk of large losses. Most notably, company stock is exempted from the diversification requirement in defined-contribution plans—largely because, at the time erisa was passed, large employers with profit-sharing plans lobbied Congress to exempt them from the diversification requirements imposed on defined-benefit plans.12 Employers are still expected to act prudently, however, in determining whether company stock is a suitable investment. Why did Congress give preferred standing to company stock? No sensible definition of prudence can accommodate a concentrated position in a single stock—especially if that stock's performance is correlated with participants' work earnings. By giving company stock this odd preferential treatment, existing law actually encourages the inclusion of company stock in 401(k) plans. From the standpoint of workers' welfare, this is perverse. A natural alternative would be to treat company stock just like every other investment, without any kind of preference. This simple change might, in and of itself, solve the problem because firms might conclude that the fiduciary risk of giving large amounts of company stock to employees is not worth bearing. In the absence of a change in the law, public-spirited firms can take some steps themselves to nudge employees to reduce exceptionally large holdings of company stock. Here is an approach that will now be familiar: Sell More Tomorrow. The idea is to solve two problems. First, even if firms recognize that company stock is not so great for employees, they do not want all or most employees to sell their stock at once, for fear that such sales will lower the stock's price. Second, firms do not want to be signaling that they think their stock is a bad investment. The Sell More Tomorrow plan gives employees the option to sell off their shares gradually over a period of time (say, three years), with the proceeds directed into a diversified portfolio. The program could be done on either an opt-in or opt-out basis. 128 MONEY Nudges Through better choice architecture, plans can help their participants on many dimensions. Attention to choice architecture has become increasingly important over the years because plans have greatly increased the number of options they offer, making it even harder for people to choose well. Defaults Historically, most defined-contribution plans did not have a default option. Participants who joined the plan would be given a list of options, with the instructions to allocate their money as they wished among the funds offered. No default option was necessary until plans began to adopt automatic enrollment, a regime that requires a default: if participants are enrolled automatically, they have to be enrolled into some specific asset allocation. Traditionally, firms have selected their most conservative investment option as the default, usually a money market account. Most specialists consider a 100 percent allocation to a money market account to be much too conservative. The combination of the low rates of return earned in these funds (barely above inflation) and the low savings rates by many employees is simply a recipe for being poor when you get old. Firms chose this option not because they thought it was smart but because they were worried about getting sued if they defaulted employees into something more sensible (but riskier). This fear was exacerbated by the reluctance of the Department of Labor to issue guidelines officially blessing (by granting a "safe harbor" status) any fund that could ever decline in value. The Department of Labor has finally issued new guidelines that are quite sensible, so the legal impediment to choosing a good default fund should no longer exist. Many good default options are available. One alternative is to offer a set of model portfolios that have varying degrees of risk. We have noted that some plan sponsors offer conservative, moderate, and aggressive "lifestyle" portfolios. All a participant needs to do is select the lifestyle fund that best fits his risk preferences. Another option available to plan sponsors is to offer plan participants "target maturity funds." Target maNAÏVE INVESTING 129 turity funds typically have a year in their name, like 2010, 2030, or 2040. A participant simply selects the fund that matches her expected retirement date. Managers of the target maturity funds select the degree of risk and gradually shift the allocation away from stocks and toward conservative investments as the target date approaches. Some vendors and plan sponsors have started to offer automated solutions for portfolio selection. In particular, some plan sponsors automatically assign participants to a target maturity fund based on a standard retirement age. Others are defaulting participants into "managed accounts," which are typically portfolios of stocks and bonds whose allocations are based on the age of the participants and possibly other information. Structuring Complex Choices A 401(k) plan is an excellent domain in which to offer a process for making decisions that fit the needs of participants who have various levels of interest and sophistication. Here is an outline of a promising approach. New enrollees would be told that if they do not want to select their own investment plan, they can choose the default fund that has been selected with some care by knowledgeable experts. This might be the managed account discussed above. Participants who want to be somewhat more involved would be offered a choice among a small set of balanced or lifecycle funds (with the intention that each participant would invest all her money in a single fund). For those who wanted to get really involved, a full menu of mutual funds would be offered, allowing sophisticated investors (or those who believe themselves to be sophisticated) the ability to invest as exotically as they choose. Many firms are starting to implement plans much like this. Expect Error To help those who would not get it together to join, we encourage automatic enrollment, which we would combine with Save More Tomorrow to help people achieve an adequate savings rate. For those who did not invest in a life-cycle fund, we would recommend offering an automatic rebalancing plan so that a participant's asset allocation would be adjusted over time. 130 MONEY Mappings and Feedback Most employees have difficulty understanding how numbers like savings rates, expected rates of return, and volatility translate into changes in their lifestyle when they are old. These abstract concepts can be brought into focus by offering translations into concepts anyone can understand. For example, one might create pictures of various housing options that would be available with alternative levels of retirement income. For the lowest outcome, the participant would be shown a very small, possibly rundown apartment. For higher outcomes, larger homes with swimming pools. These visual displays could be incorporated into regular feedback to participants about how they are doing in reaching their retirement savings goals. So a participant could be told in his annual report that he is currently headed for the hovel, but if he increases his savings rate now (or joins Save More Tomorrow), he could still get to the two-bedroom condo. Incentives The primary incentive problems in this context are possible conflicts of interest between the employer and the employee. The issues regarding company stock are a good example. The erisa laws already require firms to act in the best interest of the employees. These laws should be enforced. Forming and managing an investment portfolio over a long period of years is difficult. Most firms ask a team of internal experts, helped by outside consultants, to perform this task for the assets they manage. But individual participants typically undertake this task on their own, or with the help of a coworker or relative who may have intuition but lack training for the job. The end result is similar to what might be expected if most of us tried to cut our own hair—a mess. Most people need some help; good choice architecture and carefully selected nudges can go a long way.

8

CREDIT MARKETS

we are now borrowing more than they are saving. And it should not be surprising to learn that Human consumers are not any more sophisticated about their borrowing than they are about their investing. Consider Homer Simpson's experience when leasing a recreational vehicle called a Canyonero. canyonero salesman: Okay, here's how your lease breaks down. This is your down payment, then here's your monthly, annnnnnnnnd, there's your weekly. homer: And that's it, right? salesman: Yup . . . oh, then after your final monthly payment there's the routine cbp, or Crippling Balloon Payment. homer: But that's not for a while, right? salesman: Right! homer: Sweet!1 Homer's naïveté is less unusual, and more revealing, than it might seem. Let's examine three important lending markets—mortgages, student loans, and credit cards—to see whether some nudges might help the many Homers among us. Mortgages Once upon a time shopping for a mortgage was pretty easy. Most mortgages had a fixed rate for the life of the mortgage, typically thirty years. Most borrowers provided a 20 percent down payment. In this regime, comparing loans was a snap—just pick the loan with the lowest interest rate. This task was made especially easy with the passage of the choice-friendly Truth in Lending Act (also known as Regulation Z), which required all lenders to report interest rates the same way, using what is called the annual percentage rate (apr). At the time, the Truth in Lending Act was an excellent bit of choice architecture because it made it easy to compare loans. In the absence of a simple way, such as apr, to judge loans, evaluating various mortgage options is quite difficult. A study by Suzanne Shu (2007) finds that even mba students at a top school had difficulty picking out the best loans, and this was in a task that was much simpler than the one they would encounter in the real world. Mortgage shopping has now become much more complicated. Borrowers can choose from a variety of fixed-rate loans (for which the interest rate does not change over the life of the loan), and also numerous "variablerate" loans in which the interest rate goes up and down according to movements in the market. Borrowers might also consider such exotic products as interest-only loans, under which the borrower makes no payments toward the principal on the loan, meaning that it is never paid off unless the house is sold (with luck, at a profit) or the borrower either wins the lottery or refinances the loan. Many variable-rate mortgages are further complicated by so-called teaser rates—a low interest rate applies for a period of a year or two, after which the rate (and payments) go up, sometimes dramatically. Then there is the matter of fees, which can vary greatly; points, which are fixed payments the borrower makes in order to receive a lower interest rate; and prepayment penalties that must be paid if the loan is repaid early. In this world, choosing a mortgage makes picking a retirement portfolio look easy. And the stakes are just as big. Here as elsewhere, the addition of more options has the potential to make people better off, but this potential is realized only if they are able to do a good job of picking the loan that is best suited to their situation and preferences. How do people do in shopping for mortgages? A study by the economist Susan Woodward (2007) examined more than seven thousand loans insured by the Federal Housing Administration (fha), a government agency that insures smaller loans and allows low down payments. Woodward studied which kinds of borrowers got the best deals, and under CREDIT MARKETS 133 what circumstances, after controlling for risk and other factors. Here are some of her key findings: · African-American borrowers pay an additional $425 for their loans. Latino borrowers pay an additional $400. (The average fee for all borrowers was $3,133 on loans that averaged about $105,000.) · Borrowers who live in neighborhoods where adults have only a high school education pay $1,160 more for their loans than borrowers who live in neighborhoods where adults have a college education. · Loans made by mortgage brokers are more expensive than those made by direct lenders by about $600. · Sources of loan complexity such as points and seller contributions to closing costs (which can make comparing loans more difficult) are expensive for borrowers, and the additional cost is greater on brokered loans than on direct loans. We can take some general lessons from this analysis. When markets get more complicated, unsophisticated and uneducated shoppers will be especially disadvantaged by the complexity. The unsophisticated shoppers are also more likely to be given bad or self-interested advice by people serving in roles that appear to be helpful and purely advisory. In this market, mortgage brokers who cater to rich clients probably have a greater incentive to establish a reputation for fair dealing. By contrast, mortgage brokers who cater to the poor are often more interested in making a quick buck.* These factors are exacerbated in the segment of the market that caters to the poorest and highest-risk borrowers, the so-called subprime market. As is often the case, there are two extreme views about subprime loans. Some, particularly those left of center or in the news media, label all such loans with the derogatory term predatory. This broad brush fails to recognize the obvious fact that higher-risk loans will have to have higher interest 134 MONEY *One brief aside here: economists often argue that when the stakes go up, people will have an incentive to get expert advice. That statement is surely true, but it does not follow that they will actually ask for and get helpful advice. In the mortgage market, many people mistakenly think that the mortgage broker is providing this service, but the broker is hardly an unbiased source. In no way do we mean to single out mortgage brokers in this respect. The poor are often fleeced by people pretending to be providing a service. rates to compensate the people who lend the money. The fact that poor and risky borrowers pay higher interest rates does not make these loans "predatory." In fact, the microfinance loans in developing countries that led to a well-deserved Nobel Peace Prize for Muhammad Yunus in 2006 often come with interest rates of 200 percent or more, yet the borrowers are made better off by these loans.2 On the other side, some observers think that the hue and cry about predatory lending is based entirely on the failure of left-leaning journalists and others to understand that risky loans require higher interest rates. As usual, the truth lies somewhere between the two extremes. Subprime lending is neither all good nor all bad. The good feature of subprime lending is that it offers credit to those who could not otherwise borrow, and makes it possible for some poor or high-risk families to become homeowners (or business owners). Subprime loans also give people a valuable second chance. Subprime lenders provide funding for any large purchase. More often than not, these purchases help people achieve an American dream—better home ownership. In fact, the vast majority of subprime loans are either refinanced mortgages or home equity loans. In what sense then are subprime loans really predatory? Subprime borrowers are often unsophisticated, and they are sometimes exploited by brokers. A front-page story in the Wall Street

Journal described in some detail the behavior of one such broker, Altaf Shaikh, a onetime professional cricket player turned pushy mortgage lender.3 Shaikh, who jumped from one mortgage company to another, made a long series of loans that greatly profited him but were generally less beneficial to his customers. For the type of borrowers Shaikh favored, here is the typical pattern. The borrowers are approached by the broker, who acts like he is doing them a favor, and so they may not do much shopping. Solicitation can be in person or via mail or nearly any other medium. For example, a home-improvement contractor might stop by a house to suggest a renovation, and then conveniently refer the residents to a mortgage broker. At the follow-up meeting, the broker suggests different mortgages to the prospective borrower. Here the borrower can "choose" the interest rate, monthly payment, and number of points she wants to pay. This last choice is particularly confusing: points allow borrowers to pay a fee (an amount that is added to the loan because the borrower typically borrows CREDIT MARKETS 135 money to pay for the points) in exchange for a lower interest rate, but few borrowers are capable of figuring out whether the points are worth paying. (Hint: usually they are not.) Once the borrower agrees to a particular mortgage, the law requires that a "good-faith estimate" be presented, spelling out all the costs of the loan, including the fee being paid to the broker. Although this estimate must be shown to the borrower within three days of the initial application, it is sometimes withheld until right before the borrower signs the mortgage. At that point, the estimate will be part of a huge pile of papers that are more often shuffled than read. This defeats the whole purpose of the estimate. The same problem occurs at closing. The broker brings a stack of papers for the borrower to look through and sign. Even though these forms describe the terms and conditions of the mortgage, signing the paperwork is a formality for most people. At such a late stage, most borrowers are not in any position to rethink (or, for that matter, think). Ironically, part of this problem was brought on by good intentions. The Truth in Lending Act was originally intended to summarize the terms of the loan in clear terms. But it is hard to see "truth" when it is buried in a mountain of fine print. For high-risk loans, a Home Ownership and Equity Protection Act disclosure is supposed to give extra warning to the borrower. But the disclosure form doesn't explicitly say "high-risk," and the borrower simply needs to sign the form. As anyone who has ever bought a house knows, there are many forms to sign, and buyers often just start signing without doing much reading. Other confusing forms make it difficult for a borrower to distinguish between the loan itself and the fees involved. Mortgage forms have hundreds of lines, and the numbers that clutter the form can obscure various charges. Many of the fees aren't defined. Some borrowers do not know that they will be charged more if they pay off their mortgage ahead of time—that is, they will face a prepayment penalty. And it doesn't help that most subprime loans have variable rates that further complicate the problem of understanding the transaction. In 2007 there was an eruption of subprime foreclosures, which caused ripples throughout financial markets, prompting many government bodies to think harder about how to help. Of course markets, left alone, will solve some of the problem, because investors who had been buying up 136 MONEY subprime loans learned the hard way that the loans were riskier than they seemed. (In many ways, the mortgage brokers were deceiving the investors who bought up the loans as well as the people who borrowed the money.) But market forces did not prevent the problem from occurring, so there have been calls for more intervention. Some demand an end to predatory lending, but because loans do not come stamped "predatory," it is hard to implement any such ban without depriving many deserving but high-risk borrowers from any source of financing. And of course, we libertarian paternalists do not favor bans. Instead, we prefer an improvement in choice architecture that will help people make better choices and avoid loans that really are predatory—loans that exploit people's ignorance, confusion, and vulnerability. In fact, we think that the entire mortgage market could benefit from a major upgrade in choice architecture. The basic problem is that the old Truth in Lending Act is now hopelessly inadequate. When interest rates vary and there are myriad fees to pay, just looking at the apr is far from enough. The law professor Lauren Wilkins (2006) suggests one strategy for reform, which is to limit the set of permissible mortgages in order to make comparison easier. This would involve banning mortgages with such features as negative amortization or balloon payments; in these mortgages, large payments are due at the end because the mortgage and interest have not been fully paid over the term. The idea is that if there were fewer types of mortgages—for example, only thirty-year fixed-rate loans—then borrowers would have an easier time choosing wisely. Wilkins thinks that the costs of these exotic mortgages outweigh the benefits. Wilkins also proposes that the loan estimate must remain valid for thirty days and that the borrower must wait before purchasing a loan. Although we see some merit in this proposal, and are sympathetic with the goal of making shopping easier, Wilkins's proposal does not qualify as libertarian paternalism because it prohibits contracts that may be mutually beneficial. Variable-rate mortgages, even with teaser rates, are not inherently bad. For those who are planning to sell their house or refinance within a few years, these mortgages can be highly attractive. Instead, we think that a version of our recap plan can help. We have in mind two versions of recap in this domain. In the simplified form, mortgage lenders would be required to report lending costs in two categories: fees and interest. In a version of such a report suggested by Wilkins, all the CREDIT MARKETS 137 different types of fees would be reported, but they would be added up into a single salient number. Woodward's research finds that the people who get the best deals—by a lot!—are those who pay no fee up front. (This just means that the broker pays all the fees out of his commission. There may be occasional free lunches, but there is no such thing as a free mortgage.) The likely explanation for this result is that when the fee is zero, it is simpler for borrowers to compare terms, because the interest rate is the only thing they have to look at. The interest-rate disclosure would include the rate, of course, but also a schedule of payments over a period of years, assuming that the underlying interest rates do not change. This would ensure that borrowers at least know what their payments will be when the teaser rate ends. It would be a good idea to add some kind of worst-case scenario information so that borrowers can see how much their payments could go up in the future. Lenders would also have to provide a machine-readable detailed recap report, one that incorporates all the fees and interest rate provisions, including teaser rates, what the variable-rate changes are linked to, caps on the changes per year, and so forth. This information would allow independent third parties to offer much better advice. Our strong hunch is that if the recap data were made available, third-party services would emerge to compare lenders. Care would need to be taken that the system did not foster collusion, but we think this would be easy enough to monitor and prevent. Recap data would thus make it much easier to shop for mortgages online, which should make the mortgage market more competitive. Online shopping is especially likely to help women and minority groups. A study of automobile shopping found that women and African-Americans pay about the same amount as white males when they buy a car online, but at the dealership they pay more, even after you account for other factors, such as income.4 Student Loans The cost of going to college has been rising almost as fast as the cost of health care and rare baseball cards. At many private universities, including ours, it costs a student more than fifty thousand dollars a year in 138 MONEY tuition, room, and board. Scholarships and part-time jobs typically do not cover the cost of college. So students and their families often turn to student loans to help out. In fact, loans are a common option. About twothirds of four-year college students are in debt when they graduate. There are two kinds of loans in the marketplace: purely private loans given by financial institutions, and loans that are backed by the federal government, so-called Stafford loans. These Stafford loans are need-based. The government pays the interest on the loans while the student is in school, guarantees payment to the lender if the student defaults, and subsidizes the loans. Lenders find making these loans highly profitable. Unfortunately, student borrowers and their families face the same kinds of difficulties as subprime borrowers. Similarly misleading mail solicitations come from private lenders, aimed at a younger audience. Some of these solicitations are hilarious in their absurdity, but apparently they're effective too. For example, one of the dozens of loan flyers that our student intern received in the mail during her senior year of high school suggested that getting a loan of forty thousand dollars could be as easy as ordering a pizza, and pictured a pizza chef promising a "Decision delivered within 15 minutes!" Shopping for a student loan is nearly as complicated as looking for a mortgage. Students typically try for a federal loan because they are cheaper (a fact not mentioned by the pizza man in the ad), then look at private loans if necessary. To apply for a federal loan a student must first fill out the free application for federal student aid (fafsa). If the student has also applied for financial aid at a private college, she must also complete the College Board's financial aid profile. Each form contains more than a hundred questions that vary according to the schools involved, and filling one out takes many hours. (Some high school and college students joke that it takes longer than the college application itself.) Like a typical mortgage form, the scale of these questionnaires is overwhelming. Students are asked to answer questions about their parents' finances, even if they don't know much about them. After the forms have been filled out, the Department of Education determines how much the student's family can pay for college (called the expected family contribution). From there, the college decides on the size of the loan. Alternatively, the student can go to the private sector for a loan. By CREDIT MARKETS 139 sending proof of college enrollment to the lender, a student can receive as much money as she thinks is necessary. Unlike federal loans, this money can be used for any expenses, so direct-to-consumer loans could potentially encourage students to borrow too much and to overspend. As in the case of mortgages, where a borrower often naïvely asks advice from his mortgage broker, students and their parents have traditionally turned to their colleges' financial aid offices for advice. Of course, most such offices are helpful and honest. Alas, some of them have been no more scrupulous than the cricket player turned mortgage broker. The loan officers offer advice, all right, but instead of a well-intentioned nudge, the advice has often been a self-serving shove. Some colleges' financial aid offices have tag-teamed with lenders who had provided gifts, stock options, and "donations" to the college in order to become "preferred lenders"—a kind of "Good Housekeeping" stamp for student loans.5 Occasionally, a college's financial aid staff tells students that they may choose only lenders on a "preferred" list, even if these lenders don't necessarily provide loans in the best interest of the student. At one university, a lender was allowed to provide staff for a call center under a college's name; when students called in to ask about loans, those "unbiased" employees pushed their own company's loans. When students took out these loans, the lender kindly shared profits with the college. One might wonder why lenders are so eager to get the student loan business that they are willing to engage in practices that are at least sleazy and possibly illegal. The answer is that the combination of loan guarantee and subsidy by the government makes these loans exceptionally profitable, so lenders compete hard to get the business. Presumably, it was the hope of such competition that led the government to design the program in this partially privatized manner, in which the federal government hands out subsidies but relies on the private sector to distribute the loans. However, the competition has not focused on price. Instead, the lenders have engaged in what economists call rent-seeking activities. The idea is that if there are high profits to be made, suppliers will be willing to spend a lot of time and money to get that business. Because excess profits are available to the lenders who snag the student loan business, there are temptations to do whatever it takes to get to the head of the line. As with mortgages, this example illustrates the problem with directing 140 MONEY people to seek "expert" advice when they face difficult, high-stakes problems and are confused about what to do. If they don't just reply to the pizza ad because it is easy, but instead try to get helpful advice, they may end up with suggestions that are as self-serving as the pizza man's. The adviser they consult has a treasure—confused customers. The opportunity to fleece confused customers is valuable. There is money on the table. It is difficult to design public policies that inhibit "advisers" from taking that money. Better to inform the consumer by improving the choice architecture. If borrowers could compare loans more easily, then the price competition that was hoped for might actually emerge. One helpful nudge would be to simplify the financial aid application. The complicated format of these forms can discourage students from applying for financial aid and cause them to seek pricey direct-to-consumer loans instead. Although the Department of Education has not released a specific formula for how it determines how much aid a family should receive, an application of recap to student loans would start with cutting down the number of questions on the fafsa and making them uniform for all loans, federal and private. The fafsa application could also be combined with an annual tax return. In one ongoing Ohio study, tax professionals at H&R Block offer a fafsa software package to families likely to qualify for federal or state financial aid. This software uses the tax return to complete most of the fafsa for submission.6 A recap policy would make it much easier for students to compare various loan options offered through their school. Indeed, learning to use a student loan recap spreadsheet might be an excellent assignment in a high school math class for seniors. Another possibility would be to help families avoid loans altogether, or at least reduce the need for such loans, by helping them start saving for college earlier via college savings accounts ("529 plans"). In research in progress by Eric Bettinger, Bridget Long, and Phil Oreopoulos, eighth graders and their parents must meet with school counselors and receive a small nudge. At the meetings, families are offered the option of directly depositing money from a checking account into a college savings account each month. As an incentive, they receive one hundred dollars in savings for signing up. Through this process, families could conveniently save money for college.7 CREDIT MARKETS 141 Credit Cards The credit card is a ubiquitous feature of modern life. It is nearly impossible to function in society without one. Try checking into a hotel, renting a car, or renting a set of golf clubs without a credit card. Good luck. Credit cards serve two functions. First, they provide a mode of payment in lieu of cash, and have largely replaced checks for that purpose in face-to-face transactions—thankfully—although occasionally you still get stuck behind someone in a grocery store checkout line who wants to write a check for a $7.37 purchase. The second purpose of a credit card is to provide a ready source of liquidity if you want to spend more than you currently have in cash. Debit cards, which look just like credit cards, serve only the first function, because they are linked to a bank account and do not allow for borrowing unless linked also to a line of credit. (Warning: some debit cards offer lines of credit at high fees. If you use a debit card to borrow, you should make sure that the fees you pay are lower than they would be with a credit card.) Credit cards are blessedly convenient. Paying with a credit card is often faster than paying with cash, and lets you avoid struggling with change; digging into your pocket to find the correct change and managing the large jar of pennies at home are vexations from which you are liberated. Not to mention the frequent flyer miles! But if you are not careful, credit cards can be addicting. Consider these numbers: · The Census Bureau reported that there were more than 1.4 billion credit cards in 2004 for 164 million cardholders—an average of 8.5 cards per cardholder. · Currently, 115 million Americans carry a month-to-month credit card debt. · In 1989 the average American family owed its credit card companies $2,697; by 2007 that number had grown to about $8,000. And these figures are probably too low because they are generally self-reported. Using Federal Reserve data, some researchers suggest that American households may have an average credit card debt of $12,000. At typical interest rates of 18 percent per year, that translates into more than $2,000 a year in interest payments alone.8 142 MONEY Looking back at the problems of self-control discussed in Chapter 3, we can see how credit cards create serious problems for some people. In the pre–credit card era, households were pretty much forced to use a pay-asyou-go accounting system. That is why people used jars of money labeled according to purpose or payee. Now if you don't have the cash to fill your car up with gas, there is always your credit card. Credit cards inhibit selfcontrol in other ways. One study by Drazen Prelec and Duncan Simister (2001) found that people were willing to pay twice as much to bid on tickets to a Boston Celtics basketball game if they could pay with their credit card rather than cash. There is no telling how much money people pay with the cards in order to get those precious frequent flyer miles. And when the spending limit on one card is reached, there is always another card to use, or a new account can be opened using one of the solicitations that arrive almost daily in the mail announcing that you have been "preapproved." Can libertarian paternalism help? As with mortgages, we think this is a perfect area for recap. We suggest that credit card companies should be required to send an annual statement, both hard copy and electronic, that lists and totals all the fees that have been incurred over the course of the year. This report would serve two purposes. First, credit card users could use the electronic version of the report to shop for better deals. By knowing their precise usage and fee payments, customers would get a better sense of what they are paying for. Here is one example. One way credit card companies have slyly raised prices is by reducing the number of days you have between the time you get your bill and the day your payment is due. If you miss that payment you not only pay a penalty, but you also pay interest on all the purchases you make next month, even if you normally pay off your bill in full. For a heavy credit card user, such as a frequent business traveler, missing a five thousand–dollar payment by one day can result in an extra payment of more than one hundred dollars. Second, the report would make more salient to users just how much they are paying over the course of the year. Some credit cards now issue an annual summary of purchases, listed by category, which can help for tax preparation, but the recap requirement would force the card issuers to in CREDIT MARKETS 143 clude information on their own fees in this document. Often those fees are hidden. For example, if you make a purchase in a foreign currency, the credit card company tacks on a fee for converting the purchase into dollars (something that costs banks virtually nothing). On your recap statement you would be told how much you paid for the privilege of using your card on your vacation to Mexico. Because interest on credit cards is not deductible, there is no particular reason for users to check how much they paid in interest last year on all their credit cards, and fees are likely to be buried and ignored altogether. Imagine the wakeup call for a credit card user who is told that over the past year he paid $2,153 in interest, $247 in late fees, and $57 in currency transaction fees. Some other nudges could help as well. For example, credit cards always mention the minimum payment you can make when you receive your monthly bill. This can serve as an anchor, and as a nudge that this minimum payment is an appropriate amount.* Of course, because the minimum payments are tiny relative to the total bill, paying this amount just maximizes the interest payments over time. Credit card companies even make it hard to commit yourself to paying the card off in full each month. Try to set up an automatic payment feature with your credit card and your bank. Chances are the only default option offered is to pay the minimum payment, not the entire bill. We think that companies should be required to allow automatic payment of the full bill. We have covered a number of topics in this chapter, but the unifying message is simple. For mortgages, school loans, and credit cards, life is far more complicated than it needs to be, and people can be exploited. Often it's best to ask people to take care of themselves, but when people borrow, standard human frailties can lead to serious hardship and even disaster. Here as elsewhere, government should respect freedom of choice; but with a few improvements in choice architecture, people would be far less likely to choose badly.

9
PRIVATIZING SOCIAL SECURITY

If we were to pick a single phrase to characterize the design of the Swedish plan, it would be "pro-choice." In fact, the plan is a good example of the Just Maximize Choices strategy. Give people as many options as 9 PRIVATIZING SOCIAL SECURITY: SMORGASBORD STYLE possible, and then let them do whatever they want. At almost every stage, the designers opted for a laissez-faire approach. In particular, the plan had the following key features: 1. Participants were allowed to form their own portfolios by selecting up to five funds from an approved list. 2. One fund was chosen (with some care) to be a default fund for anyone who, for whatever reason, did not make an active choice. 3. Participants were encouraged (via a massive advertising campaign) to choose their own portfolios, rather than rely on the default fund. 4. Any fund meeting certain fiduciary standards was allowed to enter the system. Thus market entry determined the mix of funds from which participants could choose. As a result of this process, there were initially 456 (!) available funds. (As of August 14, 2007, there were 783 funds in the plan, but since inception there have been more than 1,000, so some funds come and go rather rapidly.) 5. Information about the funds, including fees, past performance, and risk, was provided in book form to all participants. 6. Funds (except for the default fund) were permitted to advertise to attract money. If Swedish citizens were all Econs, none of these design choices would be controversial. The combination of free entry, unfettered competition, and lots of choices seems great. But if Swedes are Humans, then maximizing choice may not lead to the best possible outcome. As it turns out, it didn't. The Default Fund There are two sets of issues relating to the default fund. What should be in the portfolio? And what status should it get from the government—that is, does the government want to encourage people to take up the fund, to discourage them from doing so, or what? Here are a few of the many possible options that might have been selected: A. Participants are given no choice: the default fund is the only fund offered. 146 MONEY B. A default is picked, but its selection is discouraged. C. A default is picked, and its selection is encouraged. D. A default is picked, and its selection is neither encouraged nor discouraged. E. Required choosing. There is no default option; participants must make an active choice or they forfeit their contributions. Which of these would a good choice architect select? That depends on the architect's level of confidence in the ability and willingness of the participants to do a good job of choosing portfolios on their own. Option A is hardly a nudge. It eliminates all choice, and so is inconsistent with libertarian paternalism. We don't recommend it. At the other extreme, plan designers could avoid picking a default fund entirely by forcing everyone to choose a portfolio for themselves—option E, required choosing. If the designers are confident that people will do a good job picking portfolios for themselves, then they might consider this policy. Although required choosing can be attractive in some domains, we think that the Swedish government was right not to insist on it in this particular setting.1 Inevitably some participants will fail to respond to attempts to reach them (maybe because they are out of the country, ill, preoccupied, unable to communicate, or just clueless). Cutting such people off from all benefits is harsh, and probably unacceptable as a matter of politics or principle. In any case it isn't easy to choose among more than four hundred funds; why should a government force its citizens to make that choice, when some would prefer to rely on what experts say, as captured in the default? So we are left with the three middle options. If we are to have a default option as well as other choices, should we encourage or discourage its use? Clearly there is a wide variety of choices along the continuum from strongly discouraging the default to strongly encouraging it. What's best? Option D has obvious appeal: simply designate a default but neither encourage nor discourage it. But it is an illusion to think that this alternative fully solves the problem. What does it mean to be neutral? If we notify people that the plan was designed by experts and has low fees (both true about the actual default chosen), does this constitute encouragement? We don't mean to split hairs here. Our point is simply that designers will have to PRIVATIZING SOCIAL SECURITY 147 make a decision about how to describe the default plan, and these decisions will help determine the market share this plan attracts. In analyzing the middle options, we need to know something about the competence of those who design the default and the competence and diversity of those who might depart from it. If the designers are terrific, if the default fits all, and if the choosers are likely to blunder, then it might make sense to encourage people to select the default. If the designers are essentially guessing, if the choosers know a lot, and if the situations of different choosers are relevantly different, then it might be best to err on the size of official neutrality. In any case, the Swedish plan adopted a version of plan B. Participants were actively encouraged to choose their own portfolios via an extensive advertising campaign. This advertising effort seems to have had the desired effect, because two-thirds of participants did select portfolios on their own. Participants were more likely to make active choices if they had more money at stake, and, holding money constant, women and younger participants were more likely to make active choices. (We have a theory about why women were more likely to make active choices: we think that women were less likely to lose the enrollment forms, and more likely to remember to mail them in. We admit to having no data to support this theory, and plead guilty to the possibility that we are being overly influenced—via the availability bias—by the fact that our significant others are considerably more organized than we are.) Of course, one-third of the participants ended up with the default fund, and that figure might well seem high. It was, in fact, the largest market share of any fund. But the government campaigned hard to get people to choose actively, and a sense of the impact of the campaign can be inferred by what has occurred in the years since the plan was started. The upshot is that as the government's campaign diminished in intensity, people became significantly less likely to choose their own portfolios. Here are a few details. When the plan was launched in the spring of 2000, every participant who was then in the workforce was asked to choose a portfolio. In the years following the launch, new workers (mostly young people) have joined the plan, and they were also asked to choose a portfolio. But soon after the initial enrollment period, the government 148 MONEY ended its advertising campaign encouraging participants to make an active choice. Moreover, private funds themselves greatly reduced their advertising aimed at attracting investments. Probably as a result of both these factors, the proportion of people choosing their own portfolios fell as well. For those workers joining the plan in April 2006 (the most recent enrollment period for which we have data), only 8 percent selected their own portfolios!* Because these new participants are primarily young workers, this percentage is most usefully compared with that of workers who were under age twenty-two when the plan was launched in 2000. That group chose their own portfolios 56.7 percent of the time in 2000, much more than now. Did Active Choosers Make Good Choices? Were people made better off by choosing their own portfolios? Of course, we do not have any way of knowing the preferences of individual participants, and we also do not know what assets they may be holding outside the social security system, so it is not possible for us to say anything definitive about how good a job they did picking a portfolio. But we can nonetheless learn a lot by comparing the portfolios people actively constructed with the default fund on dimensions that sensible investors should value—such as fees, risk, and performance. To make a long story short, the active choosers didn't do so great. The default fund appears to have been chosen with some care . The asset allocation is 65 percent foreign (that is, non-Swedish) stocks, 17 percent Swedish stocks, 10 percent fixed-income securities (bonds), 4 percent hedge funds, and 4 percent private equity. Across all asset classes, 60 percent of the funds are managed passively, meaning that the portfolio managers are simply buying an index of stocks and not trying to beat the market. One good thing about index funds is that they are cheap. The fees they charge investors are much lower than those charged by funds that try to beat the market.

10

SAVING THE PLANET

In recent decades, governments all over the world have been taking aggressive steps to protect the environment. Concerned about air and water pollution, the spread of pesticides and toxic chemicals, and the loss of endangered species, governments have expended significant resources, hoping to improve human health and to reduce the harmful effects of human activities on wildlife and on pristine areas. Many of their actions have done a lot of good; efforts to reduce air pollution have prevented hundreds of thousands of premature deaths and millions of illnesses as well. But many regulatory efforts have been costly and wasteful, and some of them have aggravated the very problems that they were meant to solve. Aggressive controls of new sources of air pollution, for example, can extend the life of old, dirty sources, and thus increase air pollution, at least in the short run. In recent years, the focus has shifted to international environmental problems, including depletion of the ozone layer, now controlled by a range of international agreements, which have succeeded in banning ozone-depleting chemicals. But above all, public attention is focused on climate change, which is not yet subject to effective international controls, and on which we shall have a few things to say here. Might nudges and improved choice architecture reduce greenhouse gases? Definitely; we will sketch some promising possibilities. Most of the time, governments seeking to protect the environment and 12 SAVING THE PLANET to control the harmful health effects of pollution have gone well beyond a nudge, and their steps have not been libertarian. In this domain, freedom of choice has hardly been the guiding principle. Typically regulators have chosen some kind of command-and-control regulation, by which they reject free choices and markets entirely and allow people little flexibility in promoting environmental goals. Command-and-control regulation is sometimes embodied in technological mandates, through which government effectively requires the environmentally friendly technologies that it prefers; catalytic converters for cars are one example. More often, government officials do not specify technologies, but require across-the-board reductions in emissions. They might say, for example, that in ten years, all new cars must emit 90 percent less carbon monoxide, on average, than they now do, or that power plants must not exceed certain levels of sulfur dioxide emissions. Or the government might establish a national ambient air quality standard, insisting that every state must meet it by a specified date, and must not allow pollution levels to exceed the standard (except, perhaps, rarely). In the United States, national emissions limitations imposed on major pollution sources have been the rule, not the exception. Such limitations have sometimes been effective; the air is much cleaner than it was in 1970. Philosophically, however, such limitations look uncomfortably similar to Soviet-style five-year plans, in which bureaucrats in Washington announce that millions of people have to change their conduct in the next five years. Sometimes people do change, but sometimes they don't, or the costs of making the changes turn out to be unexpectedly high, and then the bureaucrats have to go back to work. If the goal is to protect the environment, might good choice architecture be able to help? We are all too aware that for environmental problems, gentle nudges may appear ridiculously inadequate—a bit like an effort to capture a lion with a mousetrap. When the air or the water is too dirty, the standard analysis says that it is because polluters impose "externalities" (that is, harms) on those who breathe or drink. Even libertarians tend to agree that when externalities are present, markets alone do not achieve the best outcomes. Those who pollute (meaning all of us) do not pay the full costs that we impose on the environment, and those of us who are harmed by pollution (again, all of us) usually lack any feasible way to negotiate with pol184 HEALTH luters to get them to clean up their acts. People who celebrate freedom of choice are well aware that when "transaction costs" (the technical term for the costs of entering into voluntary agreements) are high, there may be no way to avoid some kind of government action. When people are not in a position to make voluntary agreements, most libertarians tend to agree that government might have to intervene. It helps to think about the environment as the outcome of a global choice architecture system in which decisions are made by all kinds of actors, from consumers to large companies to governments. Markets are a big part of this system, and for all their virtues, they face two problems that contribute to environmental problems. First, incentives are not properly aligned. If you engage in environmentally costly behavior next year, through your consumption choices, you will probably pay nothing for the environmental harms that you inflict. This is what is often called a "tragedy of the commons." Each dairy farmer has an incentive to add more cows to his herd, because he obtains the benefits of the additional cows while suffering only a fraction of the costs; but collectively the cows ruin the pasture. Dairy farmers need to find some way to avert this tragedy, perhaps through an agreement to limit the number of cows that each will be permitted to add. Similar problems plague the fishing industry. The second problem that contributes to excessive pollution is that people do not get feedback on the environmental consequences of their actions. If your use of energy produces air pollution, you are unlikely to know or appreciate that fact, certainly not on a continuing basis. Even if you know about the connection, it is probably not salient to your behavior. Those who turn up the air conditioning and leave it on for a few weeks are unlikely to think, moment-by-moment or even day-by-day, about all of the personal and social costs. We thus begin our discussion of environmental problems with these two aspects of choice architecture: incentives and feedback. Better Incentives When incentives are badly aligned, it is appropriate for government to try to fix the problem by realigning them. In the environmental area, two broad approaches have been proposed. The first is to impose SAVING THE PLANET 185 taxes or penalties on those who pollute. In the domain of climate change, a tax on greenhouse gas emissions, favored by many environmentalists (and economists too), is a simple example. The second approach is called a cap-and-trade system. In such systems those who pollute are given (or sold) "rights" to pollute in certain amounts (the "cap") and these rights are then traded in a market. Most specialists believe that such incentivebased systems as these should usually displace command-and-control regulation. We agree. Incentive-based approaches are more efficient and more effective, and they also increase freedom of choice.1 We freely acknowledge that such proposals are not original, but the fact that we agree with most economists on this issue does not seem a sufficient reason to reject the idea! (We offer some behavioral elaborations below that incorporate the fact that agents in the economy are Humans.) Furthermore, we think that this basic approach is compatible with libertarian paternalism because people can avoid paying the tax by not creating pollution. Especially when compared with command-and-control systems, economic incentives have a strong libertarian element. Liberty is much greater when people are told, "You can continue your behavior, so long as you pay for the social harm that it does" than when they are told, "You must act exactly as the government says." Companies much prefer capand-trade systems to rigid government commands, because such systems allow more freedom and impose lower costs. If a polluter wants to increase its level of activity, and hence its level of pollution, it isn't entirely blocked. It can purchase a permit via the free market. Assuming that greenhouse gases are to be regulated, American companies have been arguing for a cap-and-trade system for exactly this reason. And if the problem of climate change is to be seriously addressed, the ultimate strategy will be based on incentives, not on command-and-control. Much of the time, the best approach to pollution problems is to impose a tax on the harmful behavior and to let market forces determine the response to the increased cost. The price of the harm-producing good will go up, and consumption will decline. Of course none of us likes taxes. But raising the tax on gasoline, for example, would eventually induce drivers to buy more fuel-efficient cars, drive less, or both. As a result, emissions of carbon dioxide, the leading contributor to global warming, would decline. And if gas taxes were increased, automobile manufacturers would have 186 HEALTH plenty of incentives to develop new technologies to meet the demand for more fuel-efficient cars. The alternative cap-and-trade system is similar in spirit and approach. In the pollution context, people who reduce their pollution below a specified level are allowed to trade their "emissions rights" for cash. In one stroke, such a system creates market-based disincentives to pollute and marketbased incentives for pollution control. Such a system also rewards rather than punishes technological innovation in pollution control, and does so with the aid of private markets. Trading systems, based on market principles, are proving increasingly popular at the international level. The Kyoto Protocol, designed to control greenhouse gases, contains a trading mechanism specifically designed to decrease the costs of emissions reductions.2 These incentive-based systems have not always gained political traction—in part, we think, because they make the costs of cleaning up the environment transparent. Announcing a new fuel efficiency standard sounds misleadingly "free," whereas imposing a carbon tax sounds expensive, even if it is actually a cheaper way of achieving the same goal. One solution to the political problem of getting such bills passed may be to use some mental accounting. For example, the revenues from a carbon tax might be paired with a cut in personal tax rates, the funding of Social Security and Medicare, or the provision of universal health insurance. Similarly, the "rights" to pollute in a cap-and-trade system can be auctioned off, and the revenues used in the same way. This linking of costs and benefits might help the pill go down more easily. In the United States, the most dramatic program of economic incentives can be found in the 1990 amendments to the Clean Air Act. Pushed by President George H. W. Bush, and broadly supported by both Republicans and Democrats, the act relies on an emissions trading system for the control of acid deposition ("acid rain"). Indeed, much of corporate America was willing to accept the system on the ground that the ability to trade emissions rights would drive down the cost. With this program, Congress made a specific decision about the "ceiling" or "cap"—the aggregate emissions level—for pollutants that produced acid deposition. Polluters are explicitly permitted to trade their allowances. Because pollution reduction can be turned into cash, strong incentives are created for environmentally beneficial behavior. SAVING THE PLANET 187 The acid deposition program has turned out to be a terrific success.3 Compliance with the program has been nearly perfect. Considerable trading has occurred; an effective market in permits has developed, just as anticipated. Since enactment of the program, the price of transporting coal has been reduced dramatically because of deregulation, and the program has proved able to handle this surprise, with permits trading for far less than anticipated. As compared with a command-and-control system, the trading mechanism is estimated to have saved $357 million annually in its first five years. For its first twenty years, the mechanism was projected to save $2.28 billion annually, for an overall savings in excess of $20 billion. Indeed, it is fair to say that the acid deposition program ranks among the most spectacular success stories in all of American environmental regulation. Because the costs of the program have been so much lower than anticipated, the cost-benefit ratio seems especially good, with compliance costs of $870 million compared to estimates of annual benefits ranging from $12 billion to $78 billion—including reductions of nearly 10,000 premature deaths and more than 14,500 cases of chronic bronchitis. It is reasonable to hope that for greenhouse gases, Congress will either rely on carbon taxes or (more likely) build on the acid deposition model, using economic incentives to reduce aggregate emissions. Indeed, much attention has already been given to the possibility of creating worldwide markets in greenhouse gas emissions rights, with a cap on global emissions.4 A central advantage of such a system is that it would ensure that reductions would be made by those who could do so most cheaply—and that those with a real need for emissions licenses would pay people, perhaps especially in poor nations, who would prefer to have the money. Feedback and Information Although we think that the most important step in dealing with environmental problems is getting the prices (that is, incentives) right, we realize that such an approach is politically difficult. When voters are complaining about the high price of gasoline, it can be hard for politicians to unite on a solution that raises this price. A key reason is that the costs of pollution are hidden, while the price at the pump is quite salient. So we suggest that along with getting the prices right (or while we are waiting for 188 HEALTH the political courage to set the prices right), we should take other nudgelike steps that can help to reduce the problem in politically more palatable ways. An important and highly libertarian step would be an improvement in the process of feedback to consumers through better information and disclosure. Such strategies can improve the operation of markets and government alike, and are also far less expensive, and less intrusive, than the command-and-control approaches that national legislatures have so often favored. To be sure, many environmentalists fear that disclosure by itself will accomplish too little. They might be right. But sometimes information is a surprisingly strong motivator. Mandatory messages about risks from cigarette smoking, first established in 1965 and modified in 1969 and 1984, are perhaps the most familiar example of a disclosure policy. The Food and Drug Administration has long maintained a policy of requiring risk labels for pharmaceutical products. The Environmental Protection Agency (epa) has done the same for pesticides and asbestos. Before the phaseout of ozone-depleting chemicals, warning labels were required for products containing such chemicals. Congress requires warnings on products with saccharin. Under President Reagan, no fan of regulation, the Occupational Safety and Health Administration issued a Hazard Communication Standard (hcs). All employers must adopt a hazard-communication program—including individual training—and inform workers of the relevant risks. The hcs has made workplaces significantly safer, and, aside from mandating disclosure, it has done so without requiring employers to alter their behavior in the slightest. Some disclosure statutes are designed to trigger political rather than market mechanisms; here the goal is not to give consumers feedback on their decisions but to inform voters and their representatives. The most famous of these statutes is the National Environmental Policy Act, enacted in 1972. The principal goal of the act is to require government to compile and disclose environmentally related information before it goes forward with any projects having a major effect on the environment. The purpose of disclosure is to activate political safeguards, coming from the government's own judgments once the environmental effects are made clear, or from external pressure on the part of citizens who have learned about SAVING THE PLANET 189 those effects. The idea behind the statute is that if the public gets riled up, the government will be pressured to give some weight to environmental effects, but if the public reacts to the disclosures with a yawn, the government would be justified in doing nothing. One significant success story for disclosure requirements is the Emergency Planning and Community Right to Know Act, a law enacted by Congress in 1986 in the aftermath of the Chernobyl nuclear reactor disaster in Ukraine.5 Originally a modest and uncontroversial measure, the law was not designed to produce environmental benefits by itself. It was essentially a bookkeeping measure, intended to give the Environmental Protection Agency a sense of what was out there. The statute turned out to do a lot more. In fact, the requirement of disclosure, captured in the Toxic Release Inventory, may be the most unambiguous success story in all of environmental law. To create the Toxic Release Inventory, firms and individuals must report to the national government the quantities of potentially hazardous chemicals that have been stored or released into the environment. The information is readily available on the epa Web site to anyone who wants it. More than twenty-three thousand facilities now disclose detailed information on more than 650 chemicals, covering more than 4.34 billion pounds of onsite and off-site disposal or other releases. Users of hazardous chemicals must also report to their local fire departments about the locations, types, and quantities of stored chemicals. And they must disclose information about potential adverse health consequences. The surprising fact is that without mandating any behavioral change, this law has had massive beneficial effects, spurring large reductions in toxic releases throughout the United States.6 This unanticipated consequence suggested that all by themselves, disclosure requirements might be able to produce significant emissions reductions.*

Thompson (2007) has explored the efforts of Southern California Edison to encourage its consumers to conserve energy—and its creative, nudgelike solution. Past attempts to notify people of their energy use with emails or text messages did no good, but what worked was to give people an Ambient Orb, a little ball that glows red when a customer is using lots of energy but green when energy use is modest. In a period of weeks, users of the Orb reduced their use of energy, in peak periods, by 40 percent. That flashing red ball really gets people's attention and makes them want to use less energy. (We think it might work even better if, when energy use went over a certain threshold, the device made annoying sounds, such as cuts from ABBA's Gold: Greatest Hits.) As Thompson notes, the underlying problem is that energy is invisible, so people do not know when they are using a lot of it. The genius of the Orb is that it makes energy use visible. Emphasizing the importance of feedback, Thompson suggests that we might find a way to see our daily consumption of energy—and perhaps even to put the relevant figures in a public place, such as a Facebook page. In fact, a design firm, DIY Kyoto (based on the Kyoto Protocol, the international effort to control emissions of greenhouse gases), already sells the Wattson, a device that displays your energy use and allows you to transmit the data to a Web site, thus permitting comparisons with Wattson users elsewhere. Thompson suggests that an approach of this kind could produce "a cascade of conservation." It's not clear how many people would actually want to make their energy use public, and we don't think that we're at a stage when public officials should require people to do so. But if people want to get into a kind of competition to conserve more, who could object? The most straightforward point is that if we can find ways to make energy use visible, we'll nudge people toward reducing their energy use without mandating any such reductions. Here's a related idea: voluntary participation programs designed to assist not individual consumers but companies both large and small. With such programs, public officials do not require anyone to do anything. Instead, they ask companies whether they would be willing to follow certain standards that are expected to have desirable effects on the environment.9 The basic idea is that even in a free market, companies often fail to use the 194 HEALTH latest products, and sometimes government can help them to make money while also reducing pollution. In 1991, for example, the epa adopted its Green Lights program, which was designed to increase energy efficiency, a goal that (in the agency's view) was simultaneously profitable and good for the environment. The epa entered into a series of voluntary agreements with both for-profit and nonprofit firms (including hospitals and universities). Through these agreements, firms pledged to implement energy-saving lighting improvements. In 1992 the epa adopted a similar innovation, the Energy Star Office Products program, also intended to promote energy efficiency, but with a focus on printers, copiers, computer equipment, and appliances in general. The epa set out voluntary performance standards and allowed participating firms to use the agency's Energy Star logo. In addition, the agency publicized the cooperation of industry groups, adopted substantial media campaigns, and offered awards to companies showing particular gains in energy efficiency. One of the epa's major goals has been to show that energy efficiency is not merely good for the environment; it produces significant savings as well. But from the standpoint of standard economic theory, no such savings should be predicted. Here's why. If companies could actually save money while protecting the environment, they would already have done that. In a market economy, firms should not need the government's help to cut their own costs. Competitive pressures should ensure that those that don't cut costs soon find themselves losing money—and out of the market. In practice, however, things don't always turn out this way. Managers in firms are busy and can't pay attention to everything. To implement some change, someone in the firm has to champion the change. In most firms, managers do not think that being the guy who pushes an energy cost–saving policy is the route to the ceo office, especially when the cost savings are small relative to the bottom line. The project sounds boring and penny-pinching, and the manager who suggests it might be destined for a job in accounting rather than the president's office. In theory, the epa's programs shouldn't have worked. So much for theory. As it turned out, both programs have succeeded in promoting greater SAVING THE PLANET 195 use of low-cost energy-efficient technologies. As a result, such technologies have become far more broadly diffused than they had previously been. Because of Green Lights, cost-saving lighting programs have been adopted in numerous places. Energy Star Office Products has led to substantial improvements in energy efficiency, yielding cost savings for those who use the relevant equipment. Government accomplished all this not with a mandate but with a gentle nudge. The success of these programs offers broad lessons for environmental protection. For those especially concerned about the problem of climate change, the lesson is clear. Whether or not governments choose some kind of incentive-based system, they can help to reduce energy use, and thus reduce greenhouse gas emissions, with a nudge. Public officials are often ignorant, to be sure, but sometimes they have useful information, and companies can literally profit from it. As a result, they can both do good and do well.

11

IMPROVING SCHOOL CHOICES

In 1944 President Franklin Delano Roosevelt included "the right to a good education" in what he called a Second Bill of Rights, designed to promote "security" and suitable for a modern democracy.1 Most Americans seem to believe that children do have a right to a good education; there is a consensus on that point. One reason for that consensus is that educated people are more free. But the consensus breaks down when people explore how, exactly, to achieve that right. School choice remains an intensely polarizing issue in American politics. The case for choice was originally popularized by the great libertarian economist Milton Friedman. His argument is a simple one: the best way to improve our children's schools is to introduce competition. If schools compete, kids win. And if schools compete, those who are the least advantaged have the most to gain. Wealthy families already have "school choice," because they can send their children to private schools. If we give parents vouchers to send their children to any school they want, then we will put children from poor families more nearly on a par with their more privileged middle- and upper-class counterparts. Shouldn't poor children have the same rights that wealthy ones do? Critics of school choice argue that such programs amount, in practice, to an attack on the public school system that has helped make America great. The critics worry that in the end, public schools, which serve diverse people and allow them to be educated together, will lose both students and money. They fear that vouchers will turn out to be a subsidy to rich parents who can already afford to send their children to fancy private schools—and even worse, that public schools will end up with the kids that the private schools don't want.

As libertarians, we are strongly inclined to support the concept of school choice, because freedom is usually a good idea and because competition is likely to improve education. But an abstract preference for choice does not allow us to select any particular plan, and of course the proof is in the pudding. We have seen that the Just Maximize Choices mantra does not always lead to the best possible outcomes. So we need to ask, when it comes to schools, do more choices actually help? Since the 1970s cities around the country have experimented with choice programs, providing observers with the chance to assess the actual effects of such programs. The evidence suggests that while choice programs are hardly a panacea, they can indeed improve student performance. Carolyn Hoxby, a leading economist who has analyzed both voucher and charter school programs, finds that when facing competition, public schools produce higher student achievement per dollar spent. Test-score improvements can range from 1 to 7 percent a year depending on the school and student—and improvement is usually greatest among younger students, low-income students, and minoritygroup members.2 Even though the results suggest that school choice can and does help, we believe that the results could be significantly enhanced by helping parents make better choices on behalf of their children. Many parents simply do not make use of their options and instead just send their child to the default school (usually, but not always, their neighborhood school). And those who do make choices are sometimes ill prepared to make good ones. Because we approve of more choice, we want to focus on one important part of the school choice issue—how to create plans that put parents in a position to make sensible decisions for their children. Complex Choices and Mental Shortcuts Consider the revealing case of Worcester, Massachusetts. President Bush signed the federal No Child Left Behind law in 2001, with the goal of increasing public school accountability by mandating certain testing standards. (We put to one side the many controversial questions raised 200 FREEDOM by that law.) By June 2003 twelve of Worcester's fifty public schools had been labeled "in need of improvement" for two consecutive years, and five for three consecutive years. That summer, forty-seven hundred students, almost one-fifth the district's student population, were eligible to transfer, and eighteen hundred students had the right to collect federal money for supplemental education services. But six months later, only one student had switched schools, and only two had taken advantage of supplemental services! Worcester officials themselves were primarily responsible. True, the school system notified parents at underperforming schools about their rights under No Child Left Behind. But it also engaged in what the political scientist William Howell calls "friendly discouragement," making parents reluctant to exercise their right to choose.3 The school system qualified its language about the meaning of underperforming, stressed the limitations of the No Child Left Behind evaluation criteria, and highlighted unattractive parts of No Child Left Behind, noting that space limitations might not permit transfers to be processed. The school system also explained that it was trying to improve. For the undeterred, exercising choice was a tedious, multistage process. First, parents had to meet with their school's principal. Few did. Next, they had to attend another meeting at a school information center. The center's director said that two parents expressed interest in such a meeting. At these meetings, district officials again stressed that transfers were not always possible and that there were no guarantees about transportation or school location. And all of that was before parents had to file the transfer paperwork. Even worse, because the school district controlled access to information, tutoring service and test prep companies could not reach students without the district's blessing. The companies essentially depended on positive comments from the school district. As with a 401(k) plan, the average parents know little about their child's school, let alone all the other schools that are available. They might well stick with the status quo or ultimately make poor decisions. The trick is to promote actual freedom—not just by giving people lots of choices (though that can help) but also by putting people in a good position to choose what would be best for their children. Consider a few details. When parents pick schools, status quo bias plays a big role. The neighIMPROVING SCHOOL CHOICES 201 borhood school that one knows, failing or not, may be preferable to the unknown school half an hour away. In any case, the Byzantine nature of collecting and distributing school data makes it difficult for parents to think through their options. In Charlotte, North Carolina, for instance, parents receive a hundred-page booklet with descriptions of 190 schools written by representatives of the schools themselves, emphasizing each school's positive features. The booklet does not include information on physical locations, test scores, attendance rates, and racial composition— these are available only on the district Web site. Meanwhile, staff members at a special district-wide application center are instructed to respond to questions like "Which school is the best school?" by saying that "a good school depends on each individual child" and advising parents to talk to their children about what their needs are, and to visit the various schools in order to determine which is best for their children. Although this advice is unobjectionable, it is about as helpful as when a waiter responds to an inquiry about what is good by saying: "Everything!" A creative experiment in Charlotte shows that choices can be improved with better and simpler information.4 Charlotte gave parents the option to apply for admission at multiple public schools besides their default school. Low-income parents tended to put less weight than high-income parents on school quality, as measured by test scores, and rarely tried to enroll in higher-performing schools. A random sample of parents was selected to receive an abbreviated "fact sheet" about the schools—much in the spirit of the recap idea that we have suggested in other areas. Printed on each sheet was a complete listing of average test scores and acceptance rates, from highest to lowest, at schools available to a given child. The experimenters wanted to find out whether parents, and especially low-income parents, would choose better schools. They did. Much better ones. The parents who received the fact sheets made decisions implying that the weight they assigned to school quality (as measured by test scores) had doubled. The schools they selected had, on average, 70 percent higher test scores than the scores at their neighborhood schools. This had the effect of making their choices similar to those of families whose incomes were $65,000 a year higher. Furthermore, when children are lucky enough to switch to better schools, their performance improves considerably. The students who are lucky enough to win the lotteries held to decide who gets 202 FREEDOM to attend the popular better schools are less likely to be suspended and have higher test scores than the students who lost.5 Incentive Conflicts and Matching A good choice architect can do more than help parents achieve what is already in their own self-interest. The architect can also help reduce latent incentive conflicts between advantaged and disadvantaged parents during the choice process. Despite the attention they receive in the media, market-based programs like vouchers are available to relatively few students nationwide. One popular alternative is a policy known as controlled choice, which emerged in the wake of 1970s court rulings prohibiting busing for the purpose of achieving desegregation. The idea was to continue integration by guaranteeing students a priority space at a nearby school or a school that a sibling attended, while giving them the option to apply for enrollment somewhere else. School administrators in Boston adopted a computer algorithm designed to assign as many students as possible to their first-choice schools, while still giving priority to the neighborhood students. It is hard to know exactly how many districts use the so-called Boston system, because administrators do not always explain controlled-choice policies in detail, but some of the larger metropolitan districts that employ that algorithm or something similar include Denver, Tampa, Minneapolis, Louisville, and Seattle. (If two students applied to a school with one open seat, Seattle and Louisville broke the tie on the basis of race, a practice the Supreme Court ruled unconstitutional in 2007.) Matching as many first choices as possible sounds sensible enough, except for one problem. Picking schools in the Boston system turns out to be a complex game of strategy, with the winners reaping the spoils. How do the winners win? They lie, a little. Economists call it strategic misrepresentation. There is a mathematical (and complicated) reason why lying is a good strategy in the Boston system, but to get an intuitive feel imagine that college admissions suddenly operated on a national controlled-choice system. Schools like Harvard and Stanford would be heavily overdemanded, and IMPROVING SCHOOL CHOICES 203 locals would get preferential treatment. You would have only slightly better odds of getting into one than of winning the Powerball jackpot. (You think property in Cambridge and Palo Alto is expensive now? What if living there guaranteed your child a seat at Harvard or Stanford?) Clever parents who do not happen to live in Cambridge, but who have been dreaming of sending their child to Harvard since the diaper days, would realize the futility of listing it first. The Boston system attempts to match as many first choices as possible, so if every honest parent in America listed Harvard first, only Cambridge residents could sleep well at night. Instead of taking their chances on a long shot, parents outside Cambridge would be better served to select as their first choice a slightly less popular school such as Dartmouth or Cornell, say, where there are also fewer students nearby getting preferential treatment. In the Boston system, parents who rank a school second or third lose out to everyone who ranks it first—making it risky to use a first choice on a highly sought-after school if a child has a low priority, and a complete waste to list such a school as a second choice. Information about school demand is usually available online, giving parents an incentive to tweak rankings based on acceptance rates and where their child has priority. When the Boston system was first developed, almost no one intuited this strategy. (Only a handful of people even knew how the algorithm worked!) But over time, some parents figured out ways to gain an edge. Not surprisingly, affluent, educated parents with large social networks (they volunteer at school with other affluent, educated parents) learned the tricks first. They performed better than less affluent, less educated parents, who routinely listed an overdemanded school as a second choice, the worst mistake they could make. Who knows how many of their children lost out on access to first-rate educations because of it? The Boston system is still in place around the country, though not in Boston. In 2003 a group of economists led by Al Roth at Harvard pointed out these problems to initially skeptical Boston school administrators. After letting the economists poke around in the internal data, the administrators became convinced of their system's flaws.6 In response, they adopted the economists' new strategy-proof choice mechanism, based on one used to match hospitals and medical residents. 204 FREEDOM The mechanism does not penalize parents who are unsophisticated about the choice process, allowing them to spend time visiting schools and seeing teachers, rather than estimating the level of competition to get into each school. In return, administrators do not have to guess about parents' true preferences so that the policy can be adjusted properly based on future feedback. Nudging High Schoolers Toward College Good choice architecture doesn't need to originate with a wonkish professor and a powerful computer algorithm. It can be the brainchild of a local school official or two. In San Marcos, Texas, the school superintendent and an administrator at nearby Austin Community College were looking for a way to get more of San Marcos's largely Latino student population into college. They hit on a nudge so simple and effective it spread through the state faster than a YouTube clip. (Well, maybe not that fast.) The nudge was this: in order to graduate from San Marcos High, a student would have to complete an application to nearby Austin Community College. Because all it takes to get admitted to the community college is a high school degree and a record of having taken a standardized test, completing the application properly was tantamount to acceptance. In San Marcos, schools run on a tight budget, and two-thirds of high schoolers never experience higher education. The superintendent had no outside funding to implement the idea, so she asked her teachers and the community college for help. Students were pulled from English classes to meet with the college's staff counselors. In a smart piece of mapping, the counselors didn't try to sell the students on the high-mindedness of education. Instead, they hooked them with the universal symbol of teenage freedom: the automobile. They talked about how much more money college graduates earned compared with high school graduates, explaining it as the difference between a Mercedes and a KIA. Next, community college administrators took a standardized admissions exam to the high school and tested the students free of charge. The administrators also gave students financial aid information and had tax consultants offer weekend sessions for parents. IMPROVING SCHOOL CHOICES 205 In the end, the nudge produced big results. From 2004 to 2005 the percentage of San Marcos High students who went to Texas colleges rose 11 percentage points, to 45 percent. Now more than forty-five Texas high schools have similar programs, and schools in Florida and California have created programs modeled after San Marcos's. In Maine a state legislator is proposing a law requiring high school seniors to submit at least one college application before they graduate. We have covered a lot of territory in a short space. Milton Friedman was right: at least in the abstract, school choice is an excellent idea, because it increases freedom and offers real promise for improving education. Of course, reforms should be assessed empirically, not in the abstract. Fortunately, existing evidence suggests that school choice has considerable promise. The major problem, and our principal concern here, is that what is true for investments and prescription drugs is true for education as well: it is not enough to make lots of choices available and then hope parents choose wisely. School systems need to put parents in a position to think through their choices, and to exercise their freedom rather than to rely on the default option. Both parents and children need the right incentives. FDR's "right to a good education" is not part of the Constitution, but it has become a cultural commitment, and a few simple steps could enable many more children to enjoy that right.

12

PRIVATIZING MARRIAGE

We are hoping that the idea of libertarian paternalism will offer some new ways of thinking about many old problems. We now turn to the very old institution of marriage, and explore some of the questions that have recently been raised about marriage and same-sex relationships. We begin by offering a proposal that is highly libertarian, that would protect freedom, including religious freedom, and that should, in principle, prove acceptable to all sides. We recognize that many people, including members of many religious groups, strongly object to same-sex marriage. Religious organizations insist on their right to decide for themselves which unions they are willing to recognize, with attention to gender, religion, age, and other factors. We also know that many members of same-sex couples want to make lasting commitments to one another. To respect the liberty of religious groups while protecting individual freedom in general, we propose that marriage, as such, should be completely privatized. Under our proposal, the word marriage would no longer appear in any laws, and marriage licenses would no longer be offered or recognized by any level of government. The state would do its business, while religious organizations would do theirs. We would eliminate the ambiguity created by the fact that the word marriage now refers both to an official (legal) status and to a religious one. Under our approach, the only legal status states would confer on couples would be a civil union, which would be a domestic partnership agreement 15 PRIVATIZING MARRIAGE between any two people.* Marriages would be strictly private matters, performed by religious and other private organizations. Within broad limits, marriage-granting organizations would be free to choose whatever rules they like for a marriage conducted under their auspices. So, for example, a church could decide that it would marry only members of that church, and a scuba diving club could decide that it would restrict its ceremonies to certified divers. Instead of channeling every partnership into the same onesize-fits-all arrangement of state marriage, couples could choose the marriage-granting organization that best suits their needs and desires. Government would not be asked to endorse any particular relationships by conferring on them the term marriage. We spell out the details of how this would work below. We then turn to questions of choice architecture. Using the principles that have helped us analyze savings policies and other aspects of life, we ask: How can the state design good rules to govern contractual arrangements between domestic partners (who will sometimes also be husband and wife as a result of a private ceremony)? What Is Marriage? As a matter of law, marriage is no more and no less than an official status, created by the state and accompanied by government entitlements and mandates. When you are married, you get many material benefits, economic and noneconomic.1 State law varies, but these benefits fall into six major categories.2 1. Tax benefits (and burdens). The tax system offers big rewards to many couples as a result of marriage—at least if one spouse earns a great deal more than the other. (There can be a big marriage penalty if both spouses earn substantial incomes.) 2. Entitlements. Federal law benefits married couples through a number of entitlement programs. Under the Family and Medical Leave Act, for example, an employer must allow unpaid leave to a worker who seeks to care for a spouse; it need not do so for "partners."3 State laws often grant similar advantages to members of married couples. 216 FREEDOM *We duck the question of whether civil unions can involve more than two people. 3. Inheritance and other death benefits. A member of a married couple obtains a number of benefits at the time of death. A husband or wife can give his or her entire estate to the spouse without incurring any estate taxes. 4. Ownership benefits. Under both state and federal law, spouses may have automatic ownership rights that mere partners lack. In community property states, people have automatic rights to the holdings of their spouses, and they cannot contract around the legal rules. 5. Surrogate decision making. Members of a married couple are given the right to make surrogate decisions of various sorts in the event of the other's incapacitation. When an emergency arises, a spouse is permitted to make judgments on behalf of an incapacitated husband or wife. Partners are far less likely to obtain these benefits. 6. Evidentiary privileges. Federal courts, and a number of state courts, recognize marital privileges, including a right to keep marital communications confidential and to exclude adverse spousal testimony. To say the least, this is an immense and diverse set of benefits, and we have by no means listed them all. The benefits also tend to be fairly stable over time; recall that the status quo is powerful, and there are sharp political constraints on any effort to rethink it. But economic and material benefits of this kind hardly exhaust the meaning of marriage. Crucially, the state explicitly links these material rights and obligations to the symbolic and expressive benefits associated with the status of marriage. For many people, perhaps most, these symbolic and expressive benefits are much of what it means to be married. So long as the state grants marriage licenses, the status of "official marriage"—that is, marriage that carries with it a legal status—has immense importance. A couple that is married within a religious or other private tradition, but not with the authority of the state, lacks an important kind of validation, regardless of the strength of that couple's private commitment or the importance to them of the religious element of their marriage. To see the importance of the state license, suppose that interracial couples were told that they could have access to all of the material benefits of marriage but that they would be in a status called "civil union" rather than "marriage." Exclusion from the institution of marriage—from the official PRIVATIZING MARRIAGE 217 status—would itself be an offense to interracial couples. In fact, it would be unconstitutional. The state cannot tell members of such couples that they receive material benefits but are not allowed to enter the legal institution of marriage. For interracial couples, it would not matter if their marriages were supported and validated by private organizations. In sum: when people marry, they receive not only material benefits but also a kind of official legitimacy, a stamp of approval, from the state. Without State Licenses We can now see that insofar as it operates through the government, marriage is an official licensing scheme—and that when the state grants marriage licenses, it gives both material and symbolic benefits to the couples it recognizes. But why combine these two functions? And what is added by official use of the word marriage? Compare marriages with other kinds of partnerships. When we decided to write this book together, we had to make a set of agreements. We jointly signed a contract with our publisher, agreeing how to divide the royalty payments we would receive if anyone chose to buy the book, and we made numerous other informal agreements about how we would write the book. The legal system will protect us through copyright laws if someone tries to republish our prose (and would also provide some rules if we had gotten into a dispute leading one of us to quit the project in disgust before the book was done). However, nothing in the legal system says that we must or must not swear a solemn oath to be best friends, to eat lunch together at least once at week but no more than twice, or to forswear other collaborations. Book writing need not be monogamous. But even when our agreements are informal, and not backed by legal sanction, we take them seriously and will in all likelihood abide by them. Insofar as the state is concerned, why not handle domestic partnerships like any other business partnerships? Why not privatize? State Control of Marriage Is Anachronistic Our basic claim here is that state-run marriage makes it impossible to protect the freedom of religious organizations to proceed as they see fit 218 FREEDOM while also safeguarding the freedom of couples to make the commitments they seek without being treated as second-class citizens by the state. But we also believe that the official licensing system no longer fits modern reality. For one thing, the institution of state-run marriage has a highly discriminatory past, enmeshed as it has been in both sexual and racial inequality. This past cannot be entirely severed from the current version of the institution of marriage.4 Insofar as it operated through government, the marital institution was originally a means of government licensing of both sexual activities and child rearing. If you wanted to have sex or to have children, you were in a much better position if you had a license from the state. In fact you might well have needed that license, no less than you now need a license to drive. A state license was a way of ensuring that sexual activity would not be a crime; and it was difficult to adopt children outside of the marital relationship. But official marriage no longer has this role. Indeed, people now have a constitutional right to have sexual relationships even if they are not married—and people become parents, including adoptive parents, without the benefit of marriage. Now that marriage is not a legal precondition for having either sex or children, the state's licensing role seems less important. As a matter of history, a primary reason for the official institution of marriage has been not to limit entry but to police exit—to make it difficult for people to abandon their commitments to one another. Of course, there are good reasons for this form of policing, which can operate as a nudge or as much more. Marriage might be seen, in part, as a solution to a self-control problem, in which people take steps to increase the likelihood that their relationship will endure. If divorce is difficult, then marriages are more likely to be stable. Marital stability is usually good for children (though children can also benefit from the end of a bad marriage). Marital stability can also be good for spouses, who may benefit from protection against impulsive or destructive decisions that are detrimental both to their relationships and to their long-term welfare. Humans, as opposed to Econs, are certainly willing to consider legal protection against impulsive decisions. (If Econs have impulses, their Reflective System keeps them under control.) We can even see the legal institution of marriage as a precommitment strategy, not unlike that of Ulysses PRIVATIZING MARRIAGE 219 in approaching the Sirens, in which people knowingly choose a legal status that will protect them against their own errors. Some states have in fact experimented with an institution called covenant marriage, which makes exit extremely difficult. People can voluntarily enter into such marriages, just as they can take other steps to protect their long-term interests. But in the modern era, exit is much less rigorously policed. In most states people can leave the marital form essentially whenever they wish to do so. And it turns out that covenant marriage has made almost no difference to the institution of marriage. Only about 1–3 percent of couples choose covenant marriage when it is available, and not surprisingly, couples who choose that option tend to be religious and to have a traditional view of marriage, child rearing, and divorce.5 By and large, such couples already have the commitments and desires that would tend to produce stable marriages. It's hardly a bad thing that they can choose a form of marriage that fits their goals, and libertarian paternalists are glad that the option is available. But the relative unpopularity of covenant marriage, and the evident failure of the movement behind it, demonstrates that the noncovenant option is pretty "sticky" for nearly all couples. Increasingly, marriage is not a particularly extraordinary contract. It is dissoluble at the will of the parties, rather than a permanent status. Now that exit is neither forbidden nor rare, it is hard to contend that the official institution of marriage is essential as a way of promoting the stability of relationships. In any case, the civil union form that we endorse, along with private institutions and their diverse norms, should be able to do the desirable work in promoting such stability. Official marriage licenses also have the unfortunate consequence of dividing the world into the status of those who are "married" and those who are "single," in a way that produces serious economic and material disadvantages for the latter (and sometimes for the former). Many of these economic and material inequalities are impossible to defend. For example, is there any good reason that a person in a same-sex relationship should not be able to make medical decisions on his partner's behalf or bequeath some of his assets upon death without paying taxes? Private relationships, intimate and otherwise, might be structured in many different ways, and the simple dichotomy between "single" and "married" does not do justice to what people might choose. Indeed, that simple dichotomy is an increas220 FREEDOM ingly imprecise description of what people actually do choose. Many people are in relationships that are intimate, committed, and monogamous— but without the benefit of marriage. Many people are in marriages that are neither intimate nor monogamous. Countless variations exist. Why not leave people's relationships to their own choices, subject to the judgments of private organizations, religious and otherwise? Is Official Marriage Beneficial? Those who want to preserve official marriage, and those who are likely to be alarmed by our proposal, might be concerned with the interests of children or the interests of the more vulnerable partner (usually the woman). These are legitimate concerns. Let us take them up in sequence. Marriage has often been understood as a means of protecting children, and it should be unnecessary to say that this goal is important. But the official institution of marriage is an exceedingly crude tool for providing that protection, which could easily be ensured in better, more direct ways.6 For example, the law could do much more to ensure that absent parents provide financial help for their children. When a child's interests are involved, mandates are perfectly appropriate. Society can and does go beyond libertarian paternalism to make so-called deadbeat dads pay child support. Those who favor nudges might just add that some simple tools might help. Consider, for example, automatic enrollment (without an opt-out right in this case) of absent parents in a payment plan so that a certain amount is deducted from the relevant checking account on a monthly basis. In any case, there is no reason to think that civil unions and private arrangements, religious and otherwise, cannot provide as much protection of children as official marriage does. If children need material support, that support can be required directly through legal institutions. If children need stable homes, the question is whether an official licensing scheme with the name marriage contributes enough to family stability to be worth the candle. Maybe so, but it's hard to see any basis for a confident answer. If the concern is for dependents at risk after the dissolution of a longterm relationship, good default rules are the best place to start. A detailed literature exists on this question; some of the most helpful suggestions are PRIVATIZING

MARRIAGE 221 both libertarian and paternalist, in the sense that they maintain freedom of choice while also steering people in desirable directions.7 We shall have more to say on possible approaches shortly. For now we note only that the official institution of marriage is neither necessary nor sufficient for good default rules. From the standpoint of good choice architecture, then, a central problem with the current licensing scheme is that it is not nearly libertarian enough. Of course, we recognize that no one is forced to marry, certainly not by law. In this way, the institution of marriage is altogether different from the kinds of rigid government commands that most threaten personal freedom. When democratic societies license marriage, they are doing something very different from what they would do by requiring (say) all employers to provide a specified level of health care, or all employees to save a specified amount of money. Marriage might even seem to be a way of facilitating private choices rather than eliminating them. But the licensing scheme is not merely a device for facilitation. It is very different from the law of contract. The state does not simply permit people to marry within their religions; it does not merely enforce people's agreements. It also creates a monopoly on the legal form of marriage; imposes sharp limits on who may enter and how; and accompanies the legal form with material and symbolic benefits that it alone confers. For those who believe in liberty, this is hardly an unambiguous good. We acknowledge that many couples may benefit, in one or another way, from public statements of their commitments to each other. Many people believe that the official institution of marriage helps to secure people's commitments in a way that is both an individual and a social good. But if commitments are important, why not rely on civil unions and private institutions, including religious ones? Is government licensing with the term marriage necessary at all? Many commitments are stable without licenses from the state. People stay tied to their friends, their churches, their coauthors, and their employers for a long time. And even without a government licensing scheme or legal sanction, people take their private commitments seriously. Members of religious organizations, homeowners' associations, and country clubs all feel bound, sometimes quite strongly, by the structures and rules of such organizations. Recall that if some kind of commitment is desirable, nothing in our proposal prevents people from 222 FREEDOM making commitments through the civil union form or purely through private institutions. In this light, what is the balance sheet for official marriage? Its benefits are surprisingly low; in many ways it is an anachronism. The most that can be said is that official marriage might contribute to a kind of commitment that benefits both couples and children. On the cost side, official marriage does not do a great deal of harm. But it does produce unnecessary polarization, confusion about the relationship between state-sponsored marriage and religious marriage, and intense grappling over fundamental issues and definitions. In the current era, the most obvious difficulty is that religious organizations insist that they should be permitted to define marriage as they like, while same-sex couples insist that they should be able to make long-term commitments without having a second-class status as a matter of law. Our proposal simultaneously satisfies both of these opposing factions. The underlying problems would easily be avoided with a simple declaration that marriage should be for private institutions, not for the state, and that religious organizations would be free to set their own rules regarding who could marry. That declaration—a form of separation of church and state—would have an additional benefit, to which we now turn. Nudging Couples In our view, the official institution of marriage, and the debate over its nature and future, have deflected attention from the key question facing choice architects: What are the appropriate default rules for people who make a commitment to each other? It is here that good choice architects can make real improvements. We cannot sort out all of the complex issues in this space, but let us sketch a few proposals, which could be applied to any form of legal domestic partisanship (including marriages in their current form). Our motivation is simple: if we were starting from scratch, no sane person could possibly devise the existing system, which is so full of confusion and arbitrariness that in many states, even experienced divorce lawyers often have no idea how disputes are likely to come out. At a minimum, the choice architecture should be changed so that people can have a clearer sense of their rights PRIVATIZING MARRIAGE 223 and obligations. More ambitiously, nudges should be introduced to protect those who are most vulnerable, frequently women and above all children. As usual, the place to start is with people's actual goals and intentions. If people make explicit promises to one another, the law should generally enforce their promises. To the extent that people leave gaps or uncertainties, the law must choose a menu of default rules. Unfortunately, people are likely to need some steering when making long-term mutual commitments. As we have suggested, unrealistic optimism is at its most extreme in the context of marriage. In recent studies, for example, people have been shown to have an accurate sense of the likelihood that other people will get divorced (about 50 percent). But recall the fact that they have an absurdly optimistic sense of the likelihood that they themselves will get divorced. It's worth repeating the key finding: nearly 100 percent of people believe that they are certain or almost certain not to get divorced!8 It is in these circumstances, and in part for that reason, that people are immensely reluctant to make prenuptial agreements. Believing that divorce is unlikely, and fearing that such agreements will spoil the mood, most people simply take their chances with existing divorce law, which is (not to put too fine a point on it) a mess, often unintelligible even to specialists in the field. Also, it is sophisticated and wealthy couples who are most likely to enter into prenuptial agreements, to understand the law, and to obtain high-quality legal representation in the event of divorce. The result of all this is to leave most people vulnerable to the vagaries of chance— and to a legal system that has an astonishing degree of uncertainty. When prenuptial agreements have not been made, we believe that the relevant rules should nudge the outcome in a way that will help the weakest parties—usually women. Typically, a woman's economic prospects fall after divorce, whereas the prospects of the man increase.9 It makes sense to adopt default rules that insure against the most severe kinds of loss. As a presumption, people should be permitted to make their own provisions if that is what they wish to do. If men and women freely agree to an outcome that generally benefits men, the law should respect that agreement—and use other parts of the legal system, including the tax-andtransfer system, to help those who need it. Mandatory rules that forbid people to agree on their preferred terms are not likely to accomplish their 224 FREEDOM intended goals; people will contract around the rules by adjusting other parts of the deal. But what people wish to do is likely to be affected by the law's default rules. If the law establishes a standard practice, many people will follow it. If the default rule says that special help will be provided to those who have been the primary caretakers of the children, then that rule is likely to stick. If joint custody is the clear default rule when neither parent has been a negligent caretaker, people will have a plain understanding of what will happen on dissolution of the household. And if the default rule says that upon divorce the primary caretaker will continue as such, and receive financial assistance, that rule will also tend to stick. In this context, the stickiness of default rules can easily be enlisted to insulate the most vulnerable people from the worst outcomes. Aside from helping the vulnerable, default rules should be clear in this arena, because Humans, unlike Econs, have a self-serving bias when it comes to negotiating settlements.10 Essentially, the self-serving bias means that in difficult or important negotiations, we tend to think that both the objectively "fair" outcome and the most likely outcome is the one that is skewed in our own favor. (After the Chicago Bears play the Green Bay Packers, ask both Bears fans and Packers fans in which direction the referees were biased.) When both sides suffer from the self-serving bias, bargaining is likely to reach an impasse, and people will spend a lot of time fighting in court, sometimes ruining their lives (at least for a time). In divorce cases, emotions are running high, and each side is likely to think itself entirely in the right, and to assume that the judge will certainly see things the same way. You might think that even if spouses are subject to self-serving bias, lawyers are not, and hence lawyers should be able to deflate their clients' expectations; but in many cases, lawyers suffer from self-serving bias as well. The upshot is that where the law is unclear, long and intense disputes are likely. Both sides would benefit if they could be nudged toward a smaller range of expected outcomes, so that their expectations will have some overlap. Families facing divorce will gain if the law provides an anchor or range, helping people know what constitutes a fair or likely outcome. To achieve this goal, the best solution is to introduce something not unlike criminal sentencing guidelines—a fairly narrow range of possible outPRIVATIZING MARRIAGE 225 comes within which a judge has discretion to consider other factors. In many states, something similar is already in place, but for purposes of the self-serving bias, the rules are less helpful if people do not know about them. And research has shown that many couples entering marriage do not have anything like a clear idea of what generally happens, with respect to either child support or alimony payments, upon divorce.11 (If you are married, or plan to get married, do you know how alimony and child support are calculated in your state? Oh, never mind. There is no chance that you will get a divorce.) States should spell out clearly what range of support is generally acceptable, as a portion of income (subjected, perhaps, to upper limits). The best approach might be an explicit formula based on such factors as the ages of both spouses, their earning capabilities, the length of marriage, and so forth. Starting with the formula as an anchor, a judge could weigh other considerations such as the standard of living during the marriage, the health of the spouse seeking maintenance, the financial prospects of both sides, and other relevant factors. The reasons for any "departures" from the range would have to be clearly spelled out and limited to a small number of acceptable reasons for adjustment, because the whole goal of transparency in the process is to nudge couples toward settlement within an expected range. But let us conclude with our broader point. With respect to marriage, there are powerful arguments for privatization—for allowing private institutions, religious and otherwise, to do as they wish, subject to default rules and criminal prohibitions. We have argued that states should abolish "marriage" as such and rely on civil unions instead. If religious institutions want to restrict "marriage" to heterosexual couples, they should certainly be permitted to do exactly that. If such institutions want to limit divorce (that is, ending a "marriage"), they could do that too. The beauty of this proposal is that it would allow a wide range of experiments—increasing freedom for individuals and religious organizations alike while at the same time reducing the unnecessary and sometimes ugly intensity of current public debates.

13

The Slippery Slope

Who would oppose nudges? We are aware that hard-line antipaternalists, and possibly others, will have serious objections.1 Let us consider the possible counterarguments in sequence. We begin with those that seem to us weakest, and then turn to those that raise more complicated issues. The Slippery Slope It is tempting to worry that those who embrace libertarian paternalism are starting down an alarmingly slippery slope. Skeptics might fear that once we accept modest paternalism for savings or cafeteria lines or environmental protection, highly intrusive interventions will surely follow. They might object that if we permit information campaigns that encourage people to conserve energy, a government propaganda machine will move rapidly from education to outright manipulation to coercion and bans. The critics could easily envisage an onslaught of what seem, to them, to be unacceptably intrusive forms of paternalism. Governments that start with education might end with stiff fines and even prison terms. The case of cigarettes offers a possible example. Here we have gone from modest warning labels to much more aggressive information campaigns to high cigarette taxes to bans on smoking in public places, and a smoker would not have to be paranoid to think that the day might eventually come when cigarettes are heavily regulated or even banned altogether. Indeed, many would welcome this for cigarettes, though most would not for alcohol. Where do we stop? Sliding all the way down the slippery slope is unlikely, to be sure, but faced with the risk of overreaching, critics might think it is better to avoid starting to slide at all. We have three responses to this line of attack. The first is that reliance on a slippery-slope argument ducks the question of whether our proposals have merit in and of themselves. If our proposals help people save more, eat better, invest more wisely, and choose better insurance plans and credit cards—in each case only when they want to—isn't that a good thing? If our policies are unwise, then it would be constructive to criticize them directly rather than to rely only on the fear of a hypothetical slippery slope. And if our proposals are worthwhile, then let's make progress on those, and do whatever it takes to pour sand on the slope (assuming that we really are worried about how slippery it is). The second response is that our own libertarian condition, requiring low-cost opt-out rights, reduces the steepness of the ostensibly slippery slope. Our proposals are emphatically designed to retain freedom of choice. In many domains, from education to environmental protection to medical malpractice to marriage, we would create such freedom where it does not now exist. So long as paternalistic interventions can be easily avoided by those who seek to adopt a course of their own, the risks decried by antipaternalists are modest. Slippery-slope arguments are most convincing when it is not possible to distinguish the proposed course of action from abhorrent, unacceptable, or scary courses of action. Because libertarian paternalists retain freedom of choice, we can say, with conviction, that our own approach opposes the most objectionable kinds of government intervention. The third point is one that we have emphasized throughout: In many cases, some kind of nudge is inevitable, and so it is pointless to ask government simply to stand aside. Choice architects, whether private or public, must do something. If the government is going to adopt a prescription drug plan, some sort of choice architecture must be put in place. With respect to pollution, rules have to be established, even if only to say that polluters face no liability and may pollute with impunity. Even if states dispensed with both marriage and civil unions, contract law would have to be available to say what disbanding couples owe each other (if anything). OBJECTIONS 237 Often life turns up problems that people did not anticipate. Both private and public institutions need rules to determine how such situations are handled. When those rules seem invisible, it is because people find them so obvious and so sensible that they do not see them as rules at all. But the rules are nonetheless there, and sometimes they are not so sensible. Those who object to nudges might accept this point for the private sector. Perhaps they believe that competitive pressures can combat the worst kinds of nudges. Rental car or cell phone companies that push people in bad directions might find themselves losing customers. We have raised questions about this view, and we will raise some more; but let us put those questions to one side and focus on the slippery-slope argument for government alone. Those who make this argument sometimes speak as if government can be absent—as if the default terms that set the background come from nature or from the sky. This is a big mistake. To be sure, the default terms that now apply in any particular context might be best, in the sense that they promote people's interests overall or on balance. But that view must be defended, not assumed. And it would be odd for those who generally hold government in extremely low esteem to think that in all domains, past governments have somehow stumbled onto a set of ideal arrangements.*

In offering supposedly helpful nudges, choice architects may have their own agendas. Those who favor one default rule over another may do so because their own economic interests are at stake. When companies offer you a special rate for the first month, then automatically reenroll you in the program at a higher rate after the end of the introductory period, their primary motivation is not to save you the trouble of signing up for yourself. So let's go on record as saying that choice architects in all walks of life have incentives to nudge people in directions that benefit the architects (or their employers) rather than the users. But what conclusion should we draw from this observation? Real architects can have conflicts of interest with their clients as well, but we don't think they should stop designing buildings. Instead, we try to line up incentives when we can, and employ monitoring and transparency when we can't. One question is whether we should worry even more about public choice architects than private choice architects. Maybe so, but we worry about both. On the face of it, it is odd to say that the public architects are always more dangerous than the private ones. After all, managers in the public sector have to answer to voters, and managers in the private sector have as their mandate the job of maximizing profits and share prices, not consumer welfare. Indeed, some of those who are most suspicious of governments think that the only responsibility of private managers is to maximize share prices. As we have emphasized, the invisible hand will, in some circumstances, lead those trying to maximize profits to maximize consumer welfare too. But when consumers are confused about the features of the products they are buying, it can be profit maximizing to exploit their confusion, especially in the short run but possibly in the long run too. The invisible hand works best when products are simple and purchased frequently. We worry very little about consumers being ripped off by their dry cleaners. A dry cleaner who loses shirts or suddenly doubles prices will not be in business long. But a mortgage broker who fails to point out that the teaser rate will disappear quickly is long gone by the time the customer gets the bad news. The editors of the Economist, in a largely sympathetic treatment of libertarian paternalism, offered this cautionary note: "From the point of view OBJECTIONS 239 of liberty, there is a serious danger of overreach, and therefore grounds for caution. Politicians, after all, are hardly strangers to the art of framing the public's choices and rigging its decisions for partisan ends. And what is to stop lobbyists, axe-grinders and busybodies of all kinds hijacking the whole effort?"2 We agree that government officials, elected or otherwise, are often captured by private-sector interests whose representatives are seeking to nudge people in directions that will specifically promote their selfish goals. That is one reason that we want to maintain freedom of choice. But if private-sector interests are just following the invisible hand in furthering the interests of their customers, what's the problem?3 The more serious point is that we should be worried about all choice architects, public and private alike. We should create rules of engagement that reduce fraud and other abuses, that promote healthy competition, that restrict interest-group power, and that create incentives to make it more likely that the architects will serve the public interest. In both the public and private sectors, a primary goal should be to increase transparency. Our various recap proposals are specifically designed to make it easier for consumers to figure out how much of some service they are using and how much they are paying for it. In the environmental domain, we have suggested that disclosure can be an effective, and low-cost, monitoring device. We would love to see similar principles used to monitor governments. Require government officials to put all their votes, earmarks, and contributions from lobbyists on their Web sites. Require those determining the future of energy policy (to cite a random example) to reveal which profitmaximizing firms were invited to lend their all-too-invisible hands to the process of designing the rules. Require those determining the future of educational policy to reveal which interest groups, and which unions, gave them money in the most recent campaign. Require government agencies, not merely the private sector, to disclose their contributions to air and water pollution, and their greenhouse gas emissions. Supreme Court Justice Louis Brandeis urged that "sunlight is the best of disinfectants." Democratic governments, as well as authoritarian ones, could use a lot more sunlight.The Right to Be Wrong Skeptics might argue that in a free society, people have the right to be wrong, and it is sometimes helpful for us to make mistakes, since that is how we learn. On the first point we heartily agree, which is why we insist on opt-out rights.

If people really want to invest their entire retirement portfolio in high-tech Romanian stocks, we say go for it. But for unsophisticated choosers, there is little harm in putting some warning signs along the way. We approve of the signs at some ski areas warning novice and intermediate skiers: "Don't even think about going down this trail if you are not an expert." We worry more about poor people who were duped into taking a mortgage they would soon be unable to afford than about the investment firms that bought portfolios of those mortgages. That latter group should have known better (though better disclosure would help here, too), and they are likely to devise improved methods of evaluating the risks of loans on their own. But how much learning do you think is good for people? We do not believe that children should learn the dangers of swimming pools by falling in and hoping for the best. Should pedestrians in London get hit by a double-decker bus to teach them to "look right"? Isn't a reminder on the sidewalk better? Of Punishment, Redistribution, and Choice Some of our most extreme critics offer an objection that will strike many readers as just odd. These critics object to any forced exchanges. They don't like to take anything from Peter to give to Paul, even if Peter is very rich and Paul is very poor. They obviously oppose progressive taxes. (Well, most taxes, actually.) In the areas that concern us, these critics would disapprove of policies that explicitly benefit the weak, poor, uneducated, or unsophisticated. They would object to these policies not because OBJECTIONS 241 they lack sympathy for these groups but because they think that any help for them should come voluntarily from the private sector, such as from charities, and that government policies would come at the expense of other groups (often the strong, rich, educated, and sophisticated). They don't like any government policy that takes resources from some in order to assist others. We must confess that we do not share the view that all redistribution is illegitimate. We think that a good society makes trade-offs between protecting the unfortunate and encouraging initiative and self-help—between giving everyone a decent share of the pie and increasing the size of the pie. In our view, the optimal level of redistribution is not zero. But even those who hate redistribution more than we do should have little concern about our policies. Most of the time, nudging helps those who need help while imposing minimal costs on those who do not. If people are already saving for retirement, offering the Save More Tomorrow program will cause them no problems. If people are not smoking, or are naturally (or unnaturally) thin, campaigns to help smokers and the obese will do them little harm. Some skeptics might object that some of our proposals would require the Econs to pay something (not a lot) for programs they don't need and from which they don't benefit. But if the people who need the help are also imposing costs on society—for example, through higher health costs— then having the Econs share in the costs of helping the Humans seems like a modest price to pay. Of course, some anti-redistributive types will object to a health system that forces the rest of us to pay for those who need health care. And it is true that on a relative basis the Econs may still lose out from policies that help Humans. If Peter's happiness depends, in part, on his being richer than Paul, then anything that pulls Paul up by his bootstraps makes Peter worse off. But we think, though we admit to having no evidence to support our view, that most Peters actually take pleasure in helping out the worst-off members of society (even if the Pauls are being helped by government rather than by private charity). As for those who feel miserable if their poorest neighbors close some of the gap, they have our sympathy, but not our empathy. The most ardent libertarians have another arrow in their quiver. They are concerned about liberty and free choice rather than about welfare. For 242 EXTENSIONS AND OBJECTIONS this reason, they prefer required choosing to nudges. At most, they would like to provide people with the information necessary to make an informed choice, and then tell people to choose for themselves: no nudges! This view is reflected in the campaign by the Swedish government to get citizens to choose their own investment portfolios and the idea that for organ donations, people should be asked to make their wishes clear, without any default rule. Both policies represent a deliberate decision not to nudge. Although nudges are often unavoidable, we enthusiastically agree that required (or strongly encouraged) active choosing is sometimes the right route, and we have no problem with providing information and educational campaigns (we are professors, after all). But forced choosing is not always best. When the choices are hard and the options are numerous, requiring people to choose for themselves might be preferred and might not lead to the best decisions. Given that people would often choose not to choose, it is hard to see why freedom lovers should compel choice even though people (freely and voluntarily) resist it. If we ask the waiter to select a good bottle of wine to go with our dinner, we will not be happy if he says that we should just choose for ourselves! As for information and educational campaigns, one of the main lessons from psychology is that it is impossible for such programs to be "neutral," regardless of how scrupulously designers try to achieve that goal. So to put it simply, forcing people to choose is not always wise, and remaining neutral is not always possible. Drawing Lines and the Publicity Principle A while back Sunstein took his teenage daughter to Lollapalooza, the three-day rock festival held every year in Chicago. On Friday night a huge sign, with changing electronic messages, often showed the schedule of performances, but interspersed that information with a message saying, "drink more water." The print was large; the message was accompanied by another one: "you sweat in the heat: you lose water." What was the point of this announcement? Chicago had been in the midst of a terrible heat wave, and those who ran Lollapalooza were clearly trying to prevent the various health problems that are associated with deOBJECTIONS 243 hydration. The sign was a nudge. No one was forced to drink. But those who produced the sign were sensitive to how people think. In particular, the choice of the particular words more water was excellent. Those words were likely to be far more effective than blander alternatives, such as "drink enough water" or "drink water." The suggestion that we "lose water" cleverly invoked loss aversion on behalf of staying hydrated. (As it happens, Sunstein wished that he had seen the sign earlier; he became very thirsty during the performance of the band Death Cab for Cutie, but the crowd was so densely packed that it was impossible to go out to find water.) Now compare an imaginable alternative. Suppose that instead of having a visible "drink more water" sign, the schedules for the day were briefly and invisibly interrupted by subliminal advertising. The subliminal advertisement might say, "drink more water," "aren't you thirsty???," or "don't drink and drive"; "drugs kill" or "support your president,"; "abortion is murder" or "buy 10 copies of NUDGE." Can subliminal advertising be seen as a form of libertarian paternalism? After all, it steers people's choices, but it does not make their decisions for them. So do we embrace subliminal advertising—so long as it is in the interest of desirable ends? What limits should be placed on private or public manipulation as such? A general objection to libertarian paternalism, and to certain kinds of nudges, might be that they are insidious—that they empower government to maneuver people in its preferred directions, and at the same time provide officials with excellent tools by which to accomplish that task. Compare subliminal advertising to something just as cunning. If you want people to lose weight, one effective strategy is to put mirrors in the cafeteria. When people see themselves in the mirror, they may eat less if they are chubby. Is this okay? And if mirrors are acceptable, what about mirrors that are intentionally unflattering? (We seem to run into more of those every year.) Are such mirrors an acceptable strategy for our friend Carolyn in the cafeteria? If so, what should we think about flattering mirrors in a fast food restaurant?